CLEVELAND COPS

CLEVELAND COPS

COPS
The Real Stories They Tell Each Other

John H. Tidyman

GRAY & COMPANY, PUBLISHERS
CLEVELAND

Gray & Company, Publishers
www.grayco.com

Library of Congress Cataloging-in-Publication Data
Cleveland cops : the real stories they tell each other / [com-
piled] by John H. Tidyman.
p. cm.
1. Police—Ohio—Cleveland—Biography. 2. Police—Ohio—
Cleveland—Anecdotes. 3. Police patrol—Ohio—Cleveland—Anecdotes. 4. Crime—Ohio—Cleveland—Anecdotes. I. Tidyman, John H.
HV7911.A1C594 2004
363.2′092′277132—DC22   2004018487

ISBN 1-886228-58-2

First printing
Printed in the United States of America

This book is dedicated to the memory of William J. Spellacy, retired Cleveland police lieutenant, husband, and father of nine. I always knew Bill and his family; he and my Dad were pals. But the last dozen years of his life, he was a wonderful friend to me. Bill was a surprising and delightful intellectual, a student of history and politics, and, to me, both counselor and confidante.

I will always miss him.

Contents

Foreword

Several years ago, I joined a panel discussing safety issues in Cleveland. I was there in my role as chief of police. A minister on the panel said this: "Cleveland police officers don't live in the real world. They live in an air-conditioned climate. They leave air-conditioned offices and slide behind the wheels of air-conditioned cars. They have no contact with the people."

While I was unable to respond to him then, I knew what I wanted to say: Reverend, in your line of work, there is right and wrong, good and evil. In police work, those lines are often blurred and it sometimes becomes difficult to determine right from wrong, good from evil.

The police officers I worked with were often tossed into situations where "brave men fear to tread." Until we learn to treat others as we would be treated, the need for brave police officers will be with us.

In this book, we're allowed to listen closely as officers talk—about missing children, armed robbers, gunfights, car chases, and so many close calls. We also listen as they laugh about the fun and the funny times. One of many lessons taught between the covers of this book is the one we often forget: police officers are human.

They are ordinary people doing extraordinary work. Every day, instances of bravery and selflessness go unrecognized and unrewarded, yet they are always expected.

This book should be required reading for the mayor and members of city council, for every elected official and for every citizen. I hope that some day soon a Cleveland high school teacher will tell me, "We're using that book about your department in our civics class."

This book also provides me an opportunity to thank officers of the Cleveland Police Department and tell them that it was an honor serving with them.

— CHIEF EDWARD P. KOVACIC

Cleveland Police Department
Appointed September 1, 1959
Chief of Police 1990–1994

Introduction

The short answer to "Why write this book?" is, "Somebody had to do it and I had the time."

I had the opportunity to talk with, and listen to, and record the voices of more than five dozen Cleveland police officers. Their personal stories gave me intimate views of the men and women who served as Cleveland police officers during the second half of the twentieth century and first years of the twenty-first.

About half the officers in this book are retired and half are on duty.

Getting a retired officer to talk was not difficult; Patrolman Emil Cielec, still active in his seventies, introduced me to officers who had retired and the ball rolled. I think they were eager to talk because no one had ever asked, "Will you tell me about your life as a Cleveland police officer?"

Getting active duty officers to talk was a different story. They are justifiably wary of anyone with a reporter's notebook and tape recorder. Far more said no than said yes.

I was walking out of the Justice Center one day and approached a couple of patrolmen. When I started my pitch, one said, "Hey, you already tried to get us to talk. The answer is no." My last ditch effort, which failed, was telling them that the book would be about their lives, their careers, their department and their city. I added that there would be no sequel, and if they continued to refuse they would regret it when the book came out. (I should add that that was the first and only time I ever told a police officer what to do. On those rare occasions that I am pulled over, I get scared as hell.)

But one young officer with about ten years on the job was working security at the Cleveland Play House one night, and I asked him. He said he would get back to me. A few days later he called and said, "I checked you out. You're okay. I have a couple of stories for you."

He not only had wonderful, funny, current, scary-as-hell and often sickening stories of his work, he introduced me to other active officers. And while more officers still said no instead of yes, those who agreed shared great stories.

Cops are fascinating for many reasons, but the one that frightens and mesmerizes me is a statistic cops keep: Killed in Line of Duty.

I often asked cops, "When was the first time you were shot at?"

No officer was surprised at the question. Each thought for a moment and then started, "The first time? Oh, that was . . ."

They die of gunshot wounds suffered in shootouts with criminals, and they die of gunshot wounds suffered in situations that are benign and normal—until a gun appears.

On the day an officer dies, he starts out as he always did. Shaving and showering, kissing the kids as they leave for school, talking about the daily events with his wife . . . or maybe arguing with her and screaming at the kids. Maybe still mad at a partner for a real or imagined slight, maybe looking forward to a ball game, maybe planning to look at a new car . . . you get the idea. And before the day is done, the life that was in him when he left that morning has been drained. His body, cooling with every passing hour, lies in the coroner's office.

The chief of police and chaplain then fulfill the duty that never gets easy: They tell the survivors that the officer is dead.

Little wonder we can't understand police officers. They live in a world none of us wants to live in. One of the detectives in this book said he was told as a young officer, "It's the gun you don't see that kills you."

Another reason for this book is the way politicians, editors and news directors use cops. The streets of Cleveland, racked with poverty, drugs and racism, are more dangerous now than they have ever been, yet the men and women who seek to fight the losing battle against crime and criminals find themselves without allies in city council or in the media. Politicians never ask to go on "ride-alongs," spending a shift with officers on the street. Editors and news directors wouldn't know the smell of gunpowder or the stickiness of fresh blood.

One of many lessons I learned with this book is less than flattering: I would not have made a good police officer. I can't say exactly what it takes to be a good officer (though one description that comes to mind is "compassionate marksman"). But when you listen to cops talk at length about their job, you realize one thing for certain: it ain't easy.

While this collection of stories will entertain a lot of people, I think it should also serve as a unique Cleveland police journal. I hope it helps many of us better understand the responsibilities we place on the shoulders of our safety officers.

— John H. Tidyman

CLEVELAND COPS

1.

"That's why I became a cop."

[JOINING THE FORCE]

MARGARET DORAN
Patrol Officer, Mounted Unit

My father was Kenny Doran, Cleveland police officer. Was he crazy? You know what, I grew up most of my life without anything else to compare it to, believing that he was the norm; that what happened in our house happened in everybody's house. As I got into my teenage years, I started to take a good look and I realized that he was one of a kind. And it had a bright side and it had a dark side. But the bright side was, here is what I learned from him: every single day is precious. The ability to laugh every day. And the ability to tell the people you love that you love them, every day.

You know what? As police officers, it taught us that you never know when your last minute is going to be, and there's no time to make it up. He used to say, "You can't tell them when they're laying in the box, pal. They're already dead. They can't hear you any more. You need to tell them now, and you need to tell them every day." The words, "I love you," were a very important thing in his life, and that's what I learned from him. I learned to live, to love, to laugh, to sing, to dance, as if no one were watching, as if there were no tomorrow. And to this day—I'm 50 years old—I live my life like that every day. And that is the legacy I pass on to my children.

When I was about seven years old, I was going to go out for Halloween. And my costume was my father's police uniform. He put the old gray shirt on me and the police patch, and he put a big pillow in there so we could pick up some of the slack. And he took an old gun handle and fashioned aluminum foil on it in a holster. And he took my long, blonde hair and put it up on my head and put that police hat on me, and his badge. Then he drew a mustache

> "You can't tell them when they're lay-
> ing in the box, pal. They're already
> dead. You need to tell them now, and
> you need to tell them every day."

on me, because everybody knew that policemen were police *men*. So from the time I was seven until the last year I went out for Halloween, I went every year in a Cleveland police uniform.

He told me when I was in high school, "Pal, do you want to go to college? I'll send you to college for anything you think you want to be, except being a police officer." He said, "It's not a life I would wish on anybody." As he got older and figured out I was really going to do it, he became more and more excited. He died a year before I got on this job.

I always knew I would be a police officer. I watched my father all those years, and I grew up in a family where the police were not the bad guys. The police were not the people you were afraid of. The police were the guys that did a job nobody else could do. Even being afraid of the things that you saw probably made you a little more cautious. It didn't mean that you didn't do it. It just meant that you were a little more careful about how you did it, which kept us alive all those years.

My father was the guy who got people to the hospitals to save them from dying from gunshot wounds. My father was the guy who delivered babies. My father was the guy who, even if it was only temporary, married the common-law couple on your badge, or divorced them on his badge, depending on the situation, "Place your hands on my badge." He was the hero to me. He was always the hero. He was the good guy with the white hat.

My mother told me when I joined the department, "You know, I know this was your dream. And this is what you wanted to do. And I love you. And I'm thrilled that you got your dream. Just don't come home telling me any thrilling war stories . . . I heard enough scary stories to last a lifetime." She said, "Do we understand each other, pal?" I said, "I promise, Mom. The only thing I'm ever going to tell you is, I can't account for the other five districts, but if anything ever happens to a policewoman and it's on TV, if you didn't get a phone call from me first, it wasn't me. I don't want you to be scared to death. If something happens and I'm involved, I'm the person you're going to get the call from, okay?"

MIKE FRICK
Sergeant, Second District (retired)

I had a pretty good job but I wanted to be an attorney. So I enrolled in the Cleveland Police Cadet program. I worked part-time and went to college. I figured I'd get my college paid for. One of the jobs I had was on the telephones at the old Third District, and a patrolman told me, "Kid, see what kind of people you're going to defend." The first year I was there, I'm thinking, how can anybody defend somebody like this . . . and go home and sleep at night? Some of the crimes people commit against other people . . . myself, I couldn't defend them and sleep at night. So I went into the academy in July 1969 and stuck it out for 30 years.

TOM TUBE
Captain

I have a degree in accounting from Case Western Reserve University. I grasped onto the FBI initially. But police work ends up in your blood. Four of my uncles were policemen. They're all alive; they're all retired. My dad died when I was very young, and I grew up listening to police stories. One of my uncles said, "Take the police test. You'll be a captain in no time."

Before I came to Cleveland, I was a policeman in Olmsted Falls for a little more than a year. In Olmsted Falls, if I had to go to five people's homes, that was a busy month. I went to the Cleveland Police Academy in April 1985. I got out of the academy the Fourth of July weekend. It was a shock. Twenty runs in a shift. Rather busy.

JEFF STANCZYK
Patrol Officer, Third District

I never wanted to be a police officer. I got out of Ohio State in 1977 with a degree in wildlife biology. I wanted to be a wildlife manager. And when I was in high school, they said, "Fill out this application and go to any national park you want." They said, "Or you can go to college, come out and [do] better." I said, "Okay, fine." So I went to school, graduated, and there was not one job. I spent about $300 in resumes and sent them to every national park. I got on a list for Rocky Mountain National Park about 15 years ago, because that field filled up so quickly. I graduated two quarters late. At that time, there were no jobs.

So I was a correction officer for about 13 months for Cuyahoga County. My job was inmate supervision. They put me in a pod with 15, 20 prisoners and I made sure that they didn't damage each other. Sounds like the odds weren't good, but it doesn't matter. They know why they're there and they know why you're there. And if you conduct yourself the way you should—there was never any problems. We had a couple, but there's a knucklehead in everything you do, anywhere you go. That was the old county jail.

I took the test before I graduated. I was home on a weekend and they had a civil service test. I took it, and it took me two years. Why I took it, I can't tell you, because I never wanted to be a policeman. I thought I'd be in my little cabin, counting chipmunk feces, managing my bears, and it just didn't work out. I went to the academy in 1980.

I don't know if anybody ever knows if they've made the right career choice. I'm a fatalist. I believe it's meant for me to do this. It was meant for me to do this. And I hope it's going to be meant for me to teach school after I get out of here in a couple of years.

TOM DIEMERT
Sergeant, Fifth District (retired)

I became a policeman because I needed a job. It was 1960. I was married at the time. Three kids. I was the custodian for our apartment. I was laid off from Republic Steel—three times. I needed a job. I was an accounting clerk, working toward what they called "career development." The day I was sworn in as a policeman, I received my last unemployment check. Being a policeman would pay 80 percent of what I was making at Republic, but at least I knew I was going to get a paycheck.

PAUL BURGIO
Patrol Officer, Fourth District

I always had an interest in law enforcement, even as a kid. I just thought policemen were cool. In 1992 I was driving down Lorain Avenue around West 130th Street and I saw two police cruisers in front of a school. I thought, "This is a freaking elementary school and there're cops there." It blew my mind how bad things had gotten. And as I'm passing the school, I look, and there's four cops playing touch football with the kids. Full uniform, guns, belts, the whole nine yards, playing touch football in the schoolyard with these kids. And it just kind of—a light bulb went on. It kind of rekindled my interest in being a policeman. Two years after I took the test, I started at the academy.

JIM GNEW
Patrol Officer, SWAT

I had been drafted and ended up with the 101st Airborne. Four times I got orders for Vietnam and they were cancelled four times. I volunteered to go because all my buddies were going. The day I got out of the Army, I was talking with my Mom and Dad and I was telling them about how many of my buddies were lost in Vietnam.

My Mom says, "You know how much money I chucked into St. Jude just so I could pray every night so you wouldn't go to Vietnam?"

After I got out of the Army, I didn't know what I wanted to do. My uncle, Gene Polk, was a motorcycle cop. In fact, he was part of Halloran's Raiders. One morning I'm sleeping and he comes in my room, wakes me up and says, "C'mon, kid, you're going to sign up for the police department." And I said, "But I don't want to be a cop." And he said, "Well, that's too bad. You're going." So he stood there while I dressed, dragged me downtown and made me sign up. And that was the end of that. I went to the academy in 1969.

DANIEL LENTZ
Patrol Officer, Third District
    It's my family's profession, so to speak. My grandfather was killed in the line of duty. My father is a lieutenant; he's been on for 44 years. My brother's a police officer. My uncle is the chief of po-

---

**I grew up with an overwhelming
sense of right and wrong.**

---

lice in Cleveland Heights. Also, he's got a son who's a sergeant on the Cleveland Heights police department. I've got a cousin who's a prosecutor and my aunt is a former prosecutor. So it's kind of in the family. I grew up with an overwhelming sense of right and wrong.

BOB RAINEY
Patrol Officer, Statement Unit (retired)
    I joined the department in 1952. I retired in 1979. I joined because I liked to do the job. I always wanted to be a policeman all my life, even as a kid. I always wanted to stand outside and hold

my arms out on the street and stop traffic. So that was a big thing. Some of our kids were police officers or traffic men. I always wanted to work in traffic until I got to be a policeman—then I didn't want traffic anymore.

ELMER WALLING
Patrol Officer, Statement Unit (retired)

I got on in February 1956. I was on construction, a boilermaker, and it was feast or famine. I was looking around for jobs everywhere. They had an announcement for the test, so I went down to city hall and I signed up and I took the test. But I was working at a titanium plant on the Pennsylvania line. I was driving out there, leaving at three o'clock in the morning and working until five or six at night and driving back. I'd get home at eight or nine o'clock at night, go to bed and go back out. So they called me and said to come down, we'll give you a physical. So I went down and got on. When I started on the job, I was making $3,800 a year. And I left, after 22 years, I think I was making $15,000 or $16,000 . . . I worked two jobs my whole time, on and off.

TAMI TONNE
Sergeant, Narcotics

I was a dispatcher first. My dad told me to take that test. I was interested in what he did, but not to the point where I wanted to do it. During the first few years as a dispatcher, I decided to take the police test. He didn't encourage me at all for that.

Like I said, I was interested in what he did. That was because a lot of it came home when we were kids. He'd have informants calling our house all the time and we'd know who they were just by the sound of their voices. We'd yell, "Hey, Dad, it's Angel!" Or, it was Charlie, or whoever. After he talked with them, out he went, out the door to talk with them or do whatever he was going to do. They don't do that anymore. Police don't give out their home numbers. My dad was in the robbery squad at that time.

ROBERT CERBA
Lieutenant, Fraternal Order of Police

I became a police officer, basically, to help people. I grew up in the city of Cleveland, West Park. I went to Cleveland public schools. I was the product of Cleveland public schools busing. I got bused back in 1979, over to Robert H. Jamison Junior High, over on East 139th Street and Harvard Avenue, which was about 260-plus blocks from my house because I lived off of West 122nd Street.

When the first police exam was available, I took it. I took the test in February of 1988. In fact, I remember the day. The Browns were playing the Jets in the playoffs. I went downtown, took the test, got out of there as soon as I could because I wanted to go home and catch the game. A couple of months later, they sent out the results. I turned out to be number 3 in the city to get on the job. I felt good about it. I always feel good about tests. I do well on tests. I got five points for residency and I got 10 points for military service. And out of a possible top score of 115, I had 113 points. I scored a 98 on the test.

So they wanted to rush an academy through. They were hurting. So they were trying to put a class on as fast as possible. They started us on June 27, 1988. We went six days a week for 13 weeks. The academy has since gotten longer. They're up to 23 or 24 weeks now.

LEE ASHCROFT
Patrol Officer, Scientific Investigations Unit (retired)

Well, I'd always had a desire, since I was a child, to be a policeman. I remember on a playground—I went to school on the West Side—I remember a little girl—her first name was Patty. She had fallen off a swing and they had taken her to the hospital. I think there was an ambulance. And the police car came up. It was an old 1947 Ford hatchback. That shows you how long ago it was. And the officers wanted to know where this little girl lived, and I knew. I raised my hand. So they put me in the back of the police car and they took me to the house where the little girl lived. And ever since then I had a desire to wear a uniform and wear a badge.

I was just captivated by their gray shirts, their badges, their navy blue slacks, and what have you. So the opportunity presented itself when I got discharged from the Air Force in 1962. I took the test in 1962. Some members of my family were disappointed, because sales was in the family. And our tradition was to work with people and sell. And of course, if you're a good worker with people, you make money, if you sell a good product.

And I remember getting the results of my civil service test that I took to get on the job. I was living at home at the time. I wasn't married. I was a bachelor. And my father gave me the letter that night when he got home and he said, "What's this all about?" I hadn't, of course, told him anything about it. I said, "Well, I took the test and I came in 26th of all the people that took the test." He said, "Well, do you want to become a police officer?" I said, "Of course, I really do." He said, "Why?" I said, "Well, it's a feeling I have. Service to the community."

I was a college graduate. I graduated in 1960 from Ohio University. My degree was in history. But I always tended toward the social sciences as opposed to the physical sciences. I enjoy working with people. That goes back to my paper route. I had a *Plain Dealer* route. My brother got it in 1944. I got it in 1949, and I held it until I graduated from West Tech in 1956.

My father got over it.

TIM LEAHY
Sergeant, Third District

I was in the Coast Guard when I took the test. My father told me to take the test. He said if I liked the work, fine, and if I didn't that was fine, too. I'm glad I did. I have no regrets. My uncle was a Cleveland policeman for 37 years; my father for 43 years.

My father, Richard, was a lieutenant, and his feeling was that he should be able to go anywhere in the city and not be bothered by anyone. He used to get to work different ways. Sometimes the

Rapid Transit and a bus, sometimes he'd ride his bike all the way to the Sixth District. He was getting off the Rapid at West 150th Street and Puritas Avenue. He was coming home. There were three people standing there, and as he walked by them, one of them said, "Let's get the old man." I should mention, he looked like a farmer—jean coveralls and a hat on, listening to a headset. But he had a gun in each pocket.

As he's walking down the stairs, the guys are passing a gun back and forth and one of them takes it and comes down to rob my father. Later my father told me, "I wasn't sure which gun I was going to pull out." So he pulled out the gun in his left pocket and shot the guy three times. The guy ran up the steps and died right there. My father arrests one of the other guys but can't find the third. He stopped the Rapid, which was just about ready to leave, and he made everyone there account for one another. There was one woman who no one could account for. That was the third robber. My father thought it was three guys, but it was two guys and a woman. The two who survived were charged with involuntary manslaughter, because they were responsible for the death of the guy my father killed.

SEAN GORMAN
Patrol Officer, Ports & Harbor Unit

I became a policeman because they called me before the firemen. My dad's a fireman. I took both tests, and the police depart-

> **I became a policeman because they called me before the firemen.**

ment called me first. I was in the 108th police academy class, and we graduated in 1993. Went right to the Fourth District. The rule of thumb I was told when I first came on was that you'll see more in your first year in the Fourth District than the rest of the policemen in the city will see in five years. And you'll see more and do more in one year there than some of the guys have in their career. You just have more volume, that's all.

WILLIAM DANIEL GALLAGHER
Patrol Officer, Third District (retired)

It was a job. I came out of the service. I was looking for a job and bing, bing. Actually, I was going to go on the fire department, but all my friends were on the police department.

RICHARD SICHAU
Patrol Officer, Third District (retired)

I joined on September 1, 1959. We had seven police officers in the family, including my uncle, Edward Jennrich. The day I was sworn in, he was being buried. He was a mounted patrolman. He was patrolling Brookside Park and his horse stumbled on the wet ground and went down. He rolled over my uncle, who died a couple weeks later. He had been a policeman for 30 years.

CHESTER TORBINSKI
Lieutenant, Accident Investigation Unit

Well, I never even thought about being a policeman. I took the exam because we had a family friend who was a detective. He was an elderly guy. I came home out of the service and he said, "Take the exam. Become a policeman." I said, "Okay, okay." So, 1946 came and I didn't take the exam. And every place I went—he was Polish like myself—we'd go to a dance or to some doing, and he would be there. And he'd always be on my back, "Take the exam. Take the exam." I got tired of that. In 1948, they had another exam. So I took it. I didn't study.

I worked then for the railroad. Then I left the railroad and I went to work for U.S. Steel in the superintendent's office there. So, anyway, I took the exam just to get him off my back. Then, in 1949, things were beginning to slow up just a little bit. And one day I came home from work and my mother said, "The police were here.

They were looking for you." I said, "For me?" I'm thinking, "I didn't do anything." He left his card. And on the card it said, "Come to the Second District for an interview," on a certain date and time.

I thought, "Well, okay. I might as well go to it." So I did. There were three other policemen. It was a rude awakening. The inspector was six feet tall and well built. You could see he was strong. And the first thing he said was, "Oh, my God. What are they sending us now? You puny guys. What do you guys do, eat corn flakes or what?"

I'm thinking to myself, "Geez, what a welcome." There were four of us. There was only one that was real masculine. He weighed about 220, maybe 210, a big ex-Marine. The others were just like myself, slender, 160, 165. The inspector said, "Well, we'll see how strong you guys are." So he took an office chair, those wooden oak ones. He flipped it down, flipped it over. He grabbed a leg, flipped it right up. He just grabbed one leg. I was the third one. The two before me got it up about a third, maybe halfway. I got it up about the same distance, about halfway. We couldn't bring it up. The big kid, he struggled, but he got it up. So I'm thinking to myself, "Oh, this is a waste of time for me. If they're looking for muscle-men, I'm out."

But he asked a few questions about our service record and why we wanted to be policemen. He asked what type of work you did in the service. I was a cryptographer in China. So, that was it. He said, "Okay. I'll see you guys." And when we left, the four of us, we said, "Well, it don't look too good for us." Lo and behold, I get the notice to come in and see the doctor. I passed the physical. We were notified later on by mail to come in for swearing-in exercises at City Hall. That was September 1 of 1949. And that was it.

BILLY EVANS
Detective, Auto Theft (retired)

I guess, really, one of the things that probably made me become a policeman was that I always liked sports cars. It seems that the police used to like to stop me because I would be driving a sports car. So I said, "If you can't beat 'em, join 'em." I became a police-man September 1, 1967. My badge number was 2103.

GARY EUGENE KANE
Sergeant, Strike Force, Sixth District

I became a police officer because when I was a child of about seven or eight years old, the men that I looked up to in my life were my two uncles, my mother's brothers. They were my role models. We were at home. My uncles were there and they were eating dinner. They were eating in the kitchen and were drinking beer. And the police came to the house for something, I don't know what. But when the police came in, my uncles stuck their beer behind the curtains. They hid their beer. I wondered, why did they do that? They must be afraid of those guys. If my uncles are afraid of them, policemen are *bad*! I'm going to be a policeman. That's where it started.

I joined the department in 1979. My mother didn't like it. My stepfather didn't like it, but they didn't object. They were scared and they were nervous. They would remind me, "Policemen get shot. Policemen get hurt," and stuff like that, especially with be-

---

They were scared and they were nervous. They would remind me, "Policemen get shot. Policemen get hurt."

---

ing my mother's only son. But she would never, if I wasn't doing something wrong, she wouldn't outright object. But I know that she was against it because she kept asking me over and over, "Are you sure you want to do that?" Because if she said "no," I probably . . . I don't know. It would've been hard . . .

I decided I wanted to be a policeman when I was seven or eight years old, whatever it was. But I was small for my age. Well, I wasn't just small; I'm kind of short anyway. When I was a teenager, they used to have the height requirement of 5 feet, 8 inches. So when I graduated high school, I was probably 5 feet, 5 or 5 feet 6 at best. I graduated at 17 and thought, I'm never going to be tall enough so I don't ever have to worry about the police job.

When I was 22 I hit 5 feet, 8, and I thought, I can take the civil service test, I can get the job. I started taking law enforcement classes at community college. I was reading books and working out all the time. Of course, I worked out all the time anyway. And I took the civil service test. I always scored real high. I scored real high on the test and I scored real high [on] the physical, but I wasn't getting the job.

And when the civil service test came up for Cleveland, I said, I've been working out, I've been studying, I'm taking these tests and I'm not getting a job; I'm just going to pray on this. So I prayed and fasted from the moment they said they were going to give the test until I took the test. I prayed to be number one on the test because that way I knew I'd get a job. Because when I was doing it in the suburbs, I'd be number four and they'd hire three people. I'd be number three and they'd hire one, something like that. So this time I just said, I'll put it in God's hands. I can't quote chapter and verse, but I know that the things that you really want, you pray on it and if you really, really want it, prayer and fasting accomplishes a lot. So that's what I trusted in.

CHARLES W. UTLEY, JR.
Patrol Officer, First District

I thought making a career change was something that I needed, and I always wanted to be a police officer since I was a little kid. I sat for the exam, and two years later I got a call at home. Previous to that I was a paramedic for nine years. I don't remember a police academy class not having somebody from the division of EMS in the class. To be a paramedic, it's two years of school. And to be a police officer, you're looking at six months. I took a $10,000 pay cut to make the transition. I still haven't caught up to that. It's been three years. I'm single with no family, no kids. I can imagine what it would be like for some of the other guys who were making the jump from EMS to the department. After six months, you're at top pay as a paramedic in the city. So you go in the police academy for six months and you're making $8.50 an hour. So how do you support your family? It's not easy.

WILLIAM TELL
Commander, Sixth District (retired)

I grew up on Central Avenue. We moved there in 1952, and I always saw the police walking the beat. I was there in 1969, visiting my mother, and there was the policeman walking the beat. I remember in those days they used to put tickets on people's cars when they were parked illegally in rush hour. When he didn't ticket some cars, I asked him about it. He said he didn't want to get his hands cold.

I worked at TRW, and a guy at TRW, an inspector, came to me and told me I was going to get fired for a mistake I made on a machine. And he told me about Don McNea's police class. He said 90 percent of the people who go to his class pass the test to get on the police department. He said, "How'd you like to be a Cleveland police officer?" Well, I had to do something. McNea was a commander in the Sixth District. In addition to taking the class, he tutored me for a promotion.

KYLE STOUGES
Patrol Officer, Third District

I've always had an interest in becoming a police officer. My dad was a New York police officer and he was injured early on. He had to have screws put in his leg. He moved here to Ohio and got involved in other things. Then he started his own business. When I told him I was accepted, he was overwhelmed. He helped me interview with the FBI when I was in college, but it wasn't what I wanted to do. I wanted to be in the streets where I grew up and just be close to things. I went to St. Ignatius and was on the first state championship football team in 1988. Then Xavier University.

Now I'm finishing up at Baldwin-Wallace. My major is political science.

Not many people can say they enjoy going to work. It took a little while to get past the gung-ho attitude, to kind of settle, but my partners and I have that happy medium. I enjoy going to work. I love nights. It cuts out the middleman. You're only dealing with a certain type of person, someone who's out prowling in the night air. You don't have a lot of your model citizens roaming at three in the morning on a heavy drug corner.

ED KOVACIC
Chief (retired)

I always wanted to be a police officer. I don't know why. My father was a ward leader, and I was raised around East 96th Street and St. Clair Avenue. When I was 20, I was filling out an application for the police department. And at that time, workers at White Motors were on strike. And the police were pretty harsh during the strike.

My father asked me what I was doing and I said, "I'm filling out an application for the police department." My father said, "No son of mine will ever be a strike breaker. I'll do everything I can to keep

---

My father said, "No son of mine will ever be a strike breaker. I'll do everything I can to keep you from becoming a policeman."

---

you from becoming a policeman." So I never bothered.

I worked for the water department and I tried to sell real estate, life insurance and I failed in both of those. My wife started hollering at my father. He changed his mind because of my wife. I went down to take the test and came in 13th out of a thousand applications. I never studied for it. I just went down and took it cold and came in 13th. I turned it down the first time I got called. I was working for an insurance company and applied for a big promotion and it never came through. So the second time [the police department] called, my wife said, "This is it, Buddy. You either take it or . . ."

ROBERT LEGG
Lieutenant, Third District (retired)
I became a police officer for the job security. I had been laid off a number of times and it occurred to me that police were never laid off.

ELIAS DIAZ
Sergeant, Police Academy
I wanted to become a policeman because as a kid growing up on West 98th Street and Madison Avenue, we saw police and firemen all the time. I looked up to them. I spent five years in the Marines, then took the test. My academy class was June, 1988. My first assignment . . . I loved it, but I had no idea there'd be so much paperwork. They don't show you that on TV.

DAVID HICKS
Detective, Homicide Unit
I really don't know why I became a policeman. I never planned on it. I was born and raised in Wisconsin, a farm boy. I came to Cleveland by way of the Coast Guard. And what happened was, after I left the service, I stopped in Cleveland and I worked at a job, working in the summer at a recreation program with the City of Cleveland through a friend of mine who was in the Coast Guard.

And during that time, the police and firemen used to come over to Estabrook Recreation Center. Every Wednesday morning, they had the pool and the gym. So I used to play basketball with them and swim with them. And they talked me into taking the police test. In fact, I signed up 15 minutes before the deadline to register.

About 1,500 guys took the test and 500 of that group passed, and I was 264th on the list. I never thought anything more about it until I got a call one day. The guy said, "Are you the Dave Hicks that wants to become a policeman?" At that time, I wasn't really working anywhere. So I said, "Yeah." I went down and I started the process—the interview, the medical, the polygraph, the psychological tests. I didn't hear anything for about a month.

Then I got a call on a Friday night. He said, "So do you still want to be a policeman?" I said, "Yeah." He said, "Be down at city hall on Monday, September 1." I went down there and got sworn in, and boom, the next thing I know I was at the police academy.

2.

"If you want to survive . . ."

[THE POLICE ACADEMY]

KEVIN GRADY
Patrol Officer, Fourth District

I don't think anyone goes through the academy and enjoys it. I remember the one thing that started to get pounded into my head was how real and how dangerous this job can be. You watch a lot of videos that go around police departments and you actually see a lot of personal police videos of policemen getting shot and killed. I remember one kid in my class saying he was tired of watching them.

It was tough to watch because even a routine traffic stop isn't routine. Traffic stops are probably one of the most dangerous things to do on this job, because everybody in the car being stopped knows how a policeman is going to approach the car. They know the policeman has a gun, and a flashlight in his hand. But what does a police officer know when he approaches the car? Nothing. This job is lots of things, but one thing it isn't is routine.

PAUL FALZONE
Detective, Sixth District

Richard Wagner was the chief when I was in the academy. He came down and said, "This is what happened in the Hough riots." And he put six targets out there and just drew from the hip—*boom*! *boom*! *boom*! He emptied his gun and hit every target in the heart. We were amazed he could shoot like that.

I got on in 1967, assigned to the Sixth District. I loved going to work every day. There was a different story for every day. Some days were mundane, some days were sad. There were many, many days you'd leave work and say to yourself, "Why did I take this job?"

GARY EUGENE KANE
Sergeant, Strike Force, Sixth District

I think [the academy] was a bunch of baloney, most of it. Especially when I was in. There's too much bureaucracy. You have to have x number of hours for the domestic violence. These are the laws. You have to have these elements to have a crime. And one thing when I was in the academy, you have that cultural sensitivity. You can teach people that when you're interviewing somebody, if they're not looking you in the eye and they're looking away, there's probably some deception going on there. It's a cultural matter in our society to look somebody in the eye when you're talking to them. If they start looking away and fidgeting, they're being deceitful. But if you're talking to certain Asians, they look away and that's a sign of respect. Then if you're talking to, maybe some Eastern Europeans, they're standing too far apart. We can't be everything to everybody, is my point. I believe, when I was in school, America's supposed to be the melting pot. Everybody's trying to blend into an overall ideal. I just don't believe you can adapt to every situation for every group that wants to be recognized. That's a personal belief on my part.

PETE MIRAGLIOTTA
Patrol Officer, Fourth District

I loved the academy, but I had lots of training in the military. I had gone through a lot of police training and security training and intelligence training. I thought I was a pretty [good] student. I had a good time. I think by the time you're done with the academy, you're ready to go.

I didn't know what to expect, so I tried to keep my mouth shut.

Again, I had the benefit of being in the Marines. Going into to a new unit, I learned, shut up, keep your eyes open, pay attention to the old timers. Don't try to be cool or anything. That didn't last very long. The first day I ended up I had to restrain someone.

TOM ARUNSKI
Patrol Officer, Third District (retired)
The police academy reminded me of the military. Some of the instructors were good and some of them put me to sleep. But they definitely needed to do something to let us know how to become a policeman. If you write a ticket, what to write it for and how to read the different laws in the state of Ohio, as well as the Constitution, and what not to do. At that time, we learned first aid. There was no EMT or EMS people. We delivered babies, took shooting

> **"If you want to survive, always remember: If you think they won't do it to you, they will."**

victims to the hospital. We did it all. Us and the firemen. I remember an older guy in the academy telling me, "If you want to survive, always remember: If you think they won't do it to you, they will. If you think they won't, they will. Remember that."

WILLIAM DANIEL GALLAGHER
Patrol Officer, Third District (retired)
The police academy was at Case Western Reserve. I used to drive from the West Side all the way in to University Circle. There were about 40 in my class, approximately 5 or 6 policewomen. And it was interesting. Most of the fellows were Korean War veterans . . . Some of them had different jobs and they just took the test. The day I took the police test, I thought they were giving something away down there when I went down. It was packed.

CHARLES W. UTLEY, JR.
Patrol Officer, First District

For me personally, the academy was the single most horrifying ordeal I've ever gone through. And I never want to wish it upon another person again, ever. I struggled. It was hard on me financially. It was hard on me emotionally. A lot of other people I'm sure have had a rougher time than I did. I've never had any law enforcement experience. No one in my family had any law enforcement experience. This was all new territory for me and my family, so I didn't have anything to rely upon.

There was one other guy in the academy class that I knew, who had also come from the division of EMS. But we got split up into separate groups, so I didn't know a soul. And the one person I did know was going through the same thing I was going through. So it was kind of difficult. I really don't ever want to go through that again. I was proud and relieved when graduation day arrived.

You know the one thing joining the department gave me was a sense of brotherhood that I didn't experience when I was working with EMS. Finally, I was welcomed into a group. We got piped in by the drum and pipe corps. We were welcomed by the mayor and the council in chambers. All the brass was there, hundreds of people who I never met who were family of people who were on the job, all these people in uniform. It just makes you feel proud and part of a club.

ROBERT CERBA
Lieutenant, Fraternal Order of Police

The police academy wasn't as strenuous as boot camp. Boot camp, they pressured you. They pushed you a lot harder. Here it was mainly learning. We had some physical components where we did, what they called 13 events. We had to do a mile run in under 7 minutes, a mile-and-a-half in under 12. You had to bounce a ball off a square that they had on the wall, for hand-eye coordination. You had to do a shuttle run between two people to show that you could change directions real quick; push-ups, pull-ups, sit-ups, all the normal stuff to show that you were physically able to do the job, that you didn't have any medical problems that would preclude you.

Because sometimes people have problems and they don't say anything about them. They want to make sure your knees were okay, so they had you duck-walk around. They want to make sure that they're not bringing somebody on that a week after they get hired and get out on the streets, they're going to be off on a medical because their knee just completely blew out.

The academy was good, but there were—how can I say this and be politically correct? They taught things that they knew we weren't going to use, things that would've been better taught by actually doing the job. It's hard to put something on paper and tell people how to do it without actually doing it.

A lot of stuff that they teach you in the academy is the book way that it's supposed to be. But in police work, the book doesn't always work. The book is a nice guideline, but sometimes it doesn't cover

> **A lot of people like to see things in black and white. Unfortunately, on this job there are a billion shades of gray.**

everything. A lot of people like to see things in black and white. Unfortunately, on this job there are a billion shades of gray.

I graduated in September 1988 and went to the East Side, to the Fourth District, where we were real busy.

ANDES GONZALEZ
Commander, Third District

I was appointed to the academy in 1981. George Voinovich was the mayor and I think he had made a promise to put 300 cops on by a certain time. I guess it was getting close to that time he had to deliver. Originally I said I was going to become a cop because I couldn't find another job. I came from the Bronx and I have a relative who's a New York City policeman. Back then, the normal academy class was, I want to say, 14 or 15 weeks. But we went through the academy in seven weeks, in order to make good on that promise. It was nine or 10 hours a day, Monday through Saturday.

I graduated on July 23; we hit the streets July 24. That entire week we were just training, [working with an] FTO [field training officer], [and riding as the] third person to a car. Then after that, it was one-on-one with my partner, Jim Simone. He was my training officer. And no, he didn't get me shot. He got me beat up a couple times, and we got shot at a couple of times, but no, he never got me shot.

Jimmy, at that time, I think was on the department maybe six or seven years. I never thought I'd be a cop myself, but all of a sudden I find myself wearing a uniform, a badge, a gun and [having] a partner like Jim.

And my question to him one night was, "Jimmy, is this how it is all the time?" I should have known better at the time, because he said, "Yeah, it's like this all the time." But it's like this all the time if you work with Jim. It's not like that all the time if you work with somebody else. He was a good trainer. I have a lot of respect for Jim. He taught me a lot about police work.

ELMER WALLING
Patrol Officer, Statement Unit (retired)

Your last month in the academy you had to work with a training officer in a zone car, so they put me in the Fifth District with a policeman named Lavert Gardner. And I had the old winter blouse on and the temperature had gone way up. It was on a Saturday afternoon. I was really, really warm. And we got a call to Mt. Sinai Hospital, a victim of a shooting.

So we went down the ramp into the basement of Mt. Sinai Hospital. And when we went down in there, there was a guy still attached to the old stretchers they used to have in the wagons. They had little wheels on. They used to roll them. You'd tie them in and you'd roll them. You know, like, little stretchers. And he was laying on the floor, strapped in. And he didn't have any hair on his chest. And he had a bullet hole right by his one nipple. He was screaming, and the sweat was running off of him and it was running across the floor down into a drain. And the two policemen were off with the nurses and they were laughing and joking, or whatever.

And when I saw that, I started to pass out. It just hit me. Lavert Gardner saw me, and he grabbed me and he took me over, there was a long table and he sat me down and he went over and got me a bottle of Coke over at the machine there. And he sat in front of me and he said, "You have to learn on this job, you cannot take sides. You can't get involved in things that happen."

He said, "You see that guy laying out there on that floor?" He said, "He was in a bar on Euclid Avenue and he tried to make some guy's wife, and the guy got up and shot him. So you see, he got what he asked for." And he told me that because I was going to leave, I was going home. I was going to get a bus and the hell with this noise. So that straightened me up.

So I got up and reached over to shake his hand, and when I did, I hit the bottle of Coke and spilled it all over his uniform. And we were friends throughout my whole career. He was transferred into Homicide and I was transferred to Statements in the bureau. Lavert Gardner was always a champ. I don't know if he's even alive today.

3.

"Good job, huh?"

[NEW ON THE BEAT]

JEFF STANCZYK
Patrol Officer, Third District

My first assignment was a dead body.

Nahmar Fritz was my FTO—my field training officer. He had been on a long time. I never knew his nationality, but he had a cocked eye. He had one eye that looked away from you all the time. He was just an old-time copper. And you were asked onto *their* car. You worked general duty until somebody asked you onto their car. You never got a car. You worked different every night. So we went out and got a call . . . it was an elderly female not seen.

And we pulled up and the door was open a crack. And Fritz said, "Come on." We went in, and here, a lady had died, an older lady. She was sitting in a chair kind of slumped over. She didn't stink. She hadn't been seen in, like, two, three weeks. Nobody bothered to check until I guess the paperboy or mailman finally went up. She was slumped over in the chair.

Fritz said, "This is what you've got to do. You've got to check the body and make sure nothing went on. You know, she didn't die by getting shot or something."

And I grabbed her by the shoulder—she's sitting in this chair, and the house is freezing cold. It was like something out of a movie. There was snow in the house where it had come in, and it was like, she was stiff as a board. Not only had she stiffened up, but it was so cold, she froze. And I pulled her back, and half of her face was eaten away and it was down to the bone. I'm looking, and she fell back forward.

So we called the coroner. And Fritz is just sitting. He said, "What do you think happened to her?" I said, "Officer,"—because that's what you called them then—I said, "Officer, I don't know. She might have died from natural causes, but I can't see." She had her nightgown on, but—I don't know why only half; it looked like something out of a movie—half of her face was flesh and half of it was bone.

So the coroner came in, a couple of guys. They looked like a couple of grease monkeys. Like they just towed a car and then came here to pick up this lady. And I hear this shooting. So I'm standing at the door and I looked in.

When they pulled that woman off that chair, rats had built a nest under her and were feeding off of her. That's why it looked like a perfect line. They had that part of her body, from her rear end up; they took the flesh off of her. And these coroner guys were shooting these rats that were coming out of that chair when they removed the body. And Fritz said that you'll know why, if you see a coroner, a lot of times, they carry pistols with them. I was looking and the rats were jumping. It was like one of those big, overstuffed chairs, and that's what they were doing, living off of her.

That was my first run. I'm like, "Well, let's go home. That's enough for today."

And even now, if you go through something real bad you're just expected to move on. You make the report and you go. That's why policemen are wacky; speaking from personal knowledge.

CHESTER TORBINSKI
Lieutenant, Accident Investigation Unit

I didn't like the blood and gore at first, then I got to thinking, "It's not mine." So that's how I got over it.

I was in the Accident Unit maybe two weeks when a guy slams into a light pole at East 17th Street and Euclid Avenue. We get there fast and the driver's head was sticking out of the windshield. He came in on an angle. He was on the passenger side, but he was the driver. People were screaming, "Do something! Do something!" I pulled the victim through the windshield. And blood started squirting out five feet in the air.

This guy was laying on the ground, the blood is pumping out of

---

I didn't like the blood and gore at first, then I got to thinking, "It's not mine." So that's how I got over it.

---

his throat. I didn't know what the hell I was doing, so I just put my hand over it and I squeezed, like choking him. I was never so happy to see the wagon come. We used the paddy wagon. I was never so happy to see them come. The guys said, "Okay, we'll take over." Turned out the guy lived, but there was very little blood when his head was in there and [I should have] let them pull him out.

ROBERT LEGG
Lieutenant, Third District (retired)

I grew up believing if you treated others with respect, you would be treated the same way. That all came to a shocking end when I became a policeman. I remember the first time I pulled up to a double-parked car and said, "Sir, would you mind moving it?" He called me names I never even heard before. My ideas about respect didn't fit the work of a policeman, but I still tried to teach mutual respect to new recruits.

BILL SPELLACY
Lieutenant, Fourth District (retired)

The first time I walked a beat was in the '40s, and Skid Row was on West Superior. The captain had us in and was yelling about it and said, "Clean up the place!" I believed him and I went down there. We'd use the call box on West 3rd Street to call for a wagon.

A couple guys would bring it over. One of them said to me, "Dammit, kid, you're terrible. You're arresting all these people! What are you arresting them for?"

I said the captain told me to get everybody. The guy said, "Come on in this joint here," and he took me into a bar. He introduced me to the bartender and said, "Have a beer."

There were about 50 people in the place and I was scared to have a beer. I thought I'd lose my job. He and his partner had a couple beers and I had a Coke. Then he said, as he was getting ready to leave, "Now don't bother us, kid. We got a domino game going."

TIM LEAHY
Sergeant, Third District

My very first day on the job, I'm riding down Euclid Avenue with Ron Richley, and he's looking on the other side of the street and says, "See those two girls over there?" There were two girls in miniskirts. Ron said, "Want to meet them?" He pulls the car around and tells me, "Tell them to come over here." So I said, "Hey ladies, come on over here." Ron told them to produce some I.D. Their names were Joe and Eddie—I was shocked.

MICHAEL HANEY
Lieutenant, Sex Crimes Unit (deceased)

I was sworn in in 1946. My first regular assignment was the First District. I loved police work. We were making $150 a month. My dad gave me classic advice. He said, "Never fight. Talk your way out of it. But if there's no way out, hit hard. And often."

DANNY CONNORS
Patrol Officer, First District

I was still a rookie. We were looking for a van that was involved in a robbery. Another car found the van and pulled up behind. The guys inside kicked the back door open and opened fire on the police. One of the bullets hit the windshield where the police officer was seated. The bullet bounced off the windshield and up. If it would have gone through the windshield, it would have hit the officer right in the face. That was the first time I thought, "Oh, my God, I could get killed doing this." We caught one of the guys.

* * *

In the summer of 1994, my partner and I were touring and we saw this car. It had a busted front window and we did a rabbit test. You hit your lights and if the guy takes off, chances are good it's stolen. If the driver pulls over, you just go around him. So we did the rabbit test and sure enough he takes off.

We're flying all around the block, down Woodhill, Kennedy, Cumberland, and I'm broadcasting. This was my first real pursuit. And I'm sitting there broadcasting every street sign I see. It was funny because the guy came down East 89th Street and I'm broadcasting, "I'm going through the self-service gas station right now." A couple of times it looked like the guy was going to bail, so I have my door open. I'm ready to jump out and run. We're going about 25 miles an hour because he's slowing down, but all of a sudden the guy shuts his door and turns. Well, I don't have my door shut yet and we take the corner real sharp and I go to fall out of the car. I grab the shotgun and it holds me from going out of the car. My partner reaches over and grabs me. I came within inches of falling out.

The guy kept circling and going up and down side streets. He was going head-on with another car and he swerved toward us. As soon as he swerved right at us, my partner yelled, "Ask the boss if we have permission to fire!" I looked at him and said, "What?"

The guy had driven head-on toward another police car and forced the officers up on the sidewalk, over some garbage pails and into a wall. My partner grabbed the mike and said, "He just tried to run over a police car. He's trying to kill police officers. Do we have permission to open fire?" Over the speaker we hear, "Four-forty, go ahead." And I'm thinking, "Did he say, 'go ahead?'"

So I'm hanging out the window trying to get him in my sights and I'm thinking, "I'm a rookie. Do I shoot him or do I shoot the tires?" I've got the back of his head lined up, and then I have the tire lined up. I'm going back and forth. Did he say, "Go ahead?" I'm squeezing the trigger lightly. If you're gonna shoot, you have

---

So I'm hanging out the window trying to get him in my sights and I'm thinking, "I'm a rookie. Do I shoot him or do I shoot the tires?"

---

to watch the hammer fall. If you watch the hammer, you'll be more accurate. If you just slap at the trigger, the bullet's going to go elsewhere.

Obviously, it's not a good idea to shoot from a moving car in the first place. And you're not supposed to. It's against General Police Orders. That's why I kept asking, "Did he say, 'go ahead?'" But what he meant was, "Four-forty, go ahead—what's the request? I'm listening."

So I didn't pull the trigger and the guys ended up bailing. We caught both of them. Afterward, I was thinking, "What if I'd shot him in the back of the head?"

KEITH HAVEN
Sergeant, Strike Force, First District

I graduated from the academy in 1994. I was assigned to the First District, basic patrol. I was the third man in a car for a while. It's a way of training you after you get out of the academy. You're in the back seat with a couple veteran officers in front and you ride with them.

There was a girl who surprised a burglar at her apartment on Clifton Boulevard. She saw the guy and scared him, and she was scared, too. When she called in, she had a description of the guy. She was waiting outside in the dark when we pulled up and she comes running up to the car, pointing at me, and yelling, "That's him! That's him! You got him!" In the dark, she can't really see into the car.

And one of the officers in front gets out to open the door and show her I'm not a burglar. She was pretty frantic, yelling and screaming at me. I'm kind of shocked. He opens the door and I start to get out. And the officer said to her, "It's a policeman," and he slammed the door. And my head was in the door. Bam! I get knocked into the car. Now I got a headache and they made fun of me all night because I got my head cracked in the door.

TOM DIEMERT
Sergeant, Fifth District (retired)

Right out of the academy, I was assigned to the Sixth District, but I didn't have to show up. What I did was hit all the taverns and gambling places and just gathered information. Narcotics, gambling, prostitution, illegal liquor sales. I was plainclothes. I borrowed my buddy's car. He had a Cadillac, so I looked the part of a gambler, you know. I'd go into bars, sit there, have a few drinks, talk to whomever and gather information. I don't think anyone ever suspected me because no one ever asked if I was a cop.

I was surprised with the assignment, but I was told new guys out of the academy often got assignments like mine. It was because we were a new face. The guys who ran the cheat spots would go to court, study the officers, watch to see who's getting charged, who's there. So you have to put on a new face all the time. I did that for about six months.

LEE ASHCROFT
Patrol Officer, Scientific Investigations Unit (retired)

Three of us who went to the academy together lived in the same area off of West 25th Street. We used to drive to class together. Steve Huber was a real go-getter and he became a member of the new Tactical Unit in 1967. He was engaged to be married.

I got to work in the morning, on first shift, and they said we had a policeman killed last night out at East 88th Street and St. Clair Avenue in a dry cleaning establishment. I can't remember what it was. This would've been in May of '67—Artex Cleaners. Well, the suspect lived upstairs and he decided to burglarize the dry cleaners. He went downstairs into the driveway into the side door of the cleaners. He set off the alarm and the police were called. Well, the Tactical Unit car responded and there were three people in the car. Steve was driving.

The suspect had a .38 revolver. And way back from the dark alley he fired one shot at the police car, and the shot entered the driver's window and hit Steve in the head. And the car continued forward into the intersection into the side of a church. And that's where he came to stop, against a chain-link fence.

Well, Steve was dead instantly. He was over the steering wheel. The other two police officers bailed out. Several cars responded and an arrest was effected. And eventually the suspect went to jail for . . . he didn't get the death penalty, I don't believe. I believe he got life in prison. But I think that was really my first major case. Major, because it was a homicide—it included life and death—and because it was a classmate of mine, a very close classmate of mine.

* * *

My first case in court was with defense attorney John Patrick Butler. He chewed me up one side and down the other. My evidence was never submitted because of John Butler.

I was a rookie in 1967, in the SIU [Scientific Investigations Unit]. I went out on one of my first cases. It was at Ray's Bar at East 44th Street and St. Clair Avenue. The owner, Ray—and I don't know his last name—had an argument with a patron from long standing. The bars were open until 3:30 in the morning. And along about 3:00, he really got ticked at this man and grabbed a weapon and went around the counter and shot the man and killed him.

Well, he threw everybody out of the bar, including his barmaid. The barmaid flagged a police car down and said, "There's been a shooting at Ray's Bar down the street!" And by the time the district people got down there, there was this man in front of the bar next to a stool, laying there dead, with a revolver in his hand. Well, it looked like it was cut-and-dry, according to the owner, Ray. [The victim] pulled a gun on him and he [Ray] was defending himself and killed him.

Well, further investigation revealed that the man was shot in his side. He wasn't shot in the front, several times. And as it went to trial later on, there was a witness missing that we couldn't find, who went to West Virginia. And during this trial, this witness came back to Cleveland and accidentally saw that the trial was in motion and he said, "Oh, no. No, no, no. I remember that the man did not have his trigger finger through his trigger guard on his revolver. He had the next finger in there."

Nobody fires a weapon with their next finger, the biggest finger. They fire with their trigger finger. Well, by the time the SIU got there, which was us, they had already moved the body. And I said to myself, as I testified, I thought, "What a picture that would've made, if that finger would've been photographed in that position. There would've been no question that it was not self-defense, it was murder." Well, because they were always taught that if there's any life in the body, get him to the hospital. And that's what they did. They took him to the hospital where he was pronounced dead. But that was my first major case, was the homicide at Ray's bar.

Yeah. He wasn't thinking. He just shoved it in his hand and stuck the middle finger through the trigger and that tripped him up terribly.

When I went on the stand for that, I had dug pellets out of the wall very carefully. And I wanted to get the pellets introduced in court, the pellets that missed the seat. Well, he said, "Detective Ashcroft, what type of weapon did this come from?" And I said, "Well, it came from a revolver."

Obviously, Ray had a revolver. And he said, "A revolver?" And of course, all this time, John's walking to the back of the courtroom and his voice is getting louder. And he turns around and he said,

"Are you sure this is from a revolver? It couldn't be from a pistol?" A pistol is an automatic. And I said, "Well, no, just the opposite."

I said, "It was from an automatic." Actually, it was the opposite. He said, "Are you sure this couldn't have come from a revolver?" I said, "Oh no, if you look at the cartridge, you could see where the ejector on an automatic picks the cartridge up and flings it out of the portion that holds the barrel." And he said, "Let me get this straight now. You can't fire an automatic round from a revolver?"

Well, I should've said, "I'm not sure about that, but if you wait, we can get a forensic technician in here to testify." But, no, I was the rookie. I knew all there was to know about weapons. Well, that was it. My pellets were thrown right out. I think the weapon that Ray had was an automatic. I think he used an automatic and he definitely put a revolver in the hand of the deceased.

Ray was found guilty, by the way, and sentenced to the penitentiary.

MICHAEL DUGAN
Captain (retired), Cleveland; Chief of Police, Independence

My very first day I went to the basement of the station where you would normally meet your shift of radio dispatchers. At this time, a good portion of them were sworn police officers. You would go up together as a group, relieve the dispatchers on the telephones and the consoles, and they would go home.

I was waiting, and there was hardly anybody there, it's five minutes before shift, and an old time lieutenant comes down. I said, "Lou, I think we've got some problems. It's kind of like you and me and I'm the new guy here, and none of our dispatchers or officers are here." He said, "No problem. Follow me."

I quickly paraded behind the lieutenant, across Payne Avenue to a place called Lubeck's Casino. The lieutenant gave out with a loud whistle after putting his fingers in his mouth. Then he yelled, "Time to go to work." And we had our whole shift follow us, almost like little ducks marching across Payne Avenue.

BRENDA BROWN

Police Academy

My first assignment—you're talking about many, many moons ago—I was assigned to the Third District. I was one of the first women on the streets. I remember one of the guys I worked with. He told me, "I don't like niggers. As far as I'm concerned, all blacks are niggers." I said, "Your opinion's your opinion." We worked together. We turned out to be the best of friends.

MARGARET DORAN

Patrol Officer, Mounted Unit

My first assignment was basic patrol in the Second District. Not my first day on the job, but probably my second day, I was assigned to a total stranger at roll call. That's how it's going to go. This guy is going to be one of my many field training officers, a Hispanic policeman. And I had my briefcase and my hat on and my shoes are shiny, and I'm ready to go. I follow him out to the police car. I don't say one single word. I actually figured my job was to learn from every police officer that I rode with. If I was going to be my very best, I had to keep my big Irish mouth shut, and oh, perhaps listen. So even if I learned good stuff or bad stuff, even if I only learned what I didn't want to do as a police officer, I was going to learn something from everybody I came into contact with on this job.

I throw my briefcase in the backseat. I got my little notebook. I slide in the passenger side. Because when you're a rookie, the senior officer drives and your job is to write for a long time, years. Your job is to sit there and do all the reports for years, because that's how you learn. So I sit down in the front seat with my notebook ready and my pen, and this guy hadn't even introduced himself to me. There was dead silence in the front seat of that police car. He hadn't even turned on the engine yet. And finally after a few minutes, he broke the silence and he said, "I'm just going to tell you one thing up front. I'm going to be honest with you. I don't like working with women and I don't believe they belong on this job. I just want to tell you up front so you know where you stand."

I finally looked at this policeman and I said, "I know you're not going to understand what I'm going to tell you. Here goes. Al-

---

He said, "I'm just going to tell you one thing up front. I don't like working with women and I don't believe they belong on this job."

---

though I don't like the content of what you just told me, I fiercely admire the balls that it takes to say it out loud. I'd rather have you tell me how you really feel to my face, then smile to my face and call me 'asshole' behind my back." I said, "Now, I don't think I've been out here long enough for either one of us to know what it is I'm going to turn out to be. I would hope for the very best, but I honestly don't know."

I said, "Do you think you're a good policeman?" He said, "Yeah." I said, "Do you think you're a real good policeman?" He said, "Yeah." I said, "Fine. Do the fair thing. Teach me everything you know about what it takes to be a good cop. And then if I fall on my face, then so be it. Then kick me in my ass and tell me I need to get out of here. But give me a fair shot at it and let's see what it is I'm going to turn out to be."

I was working with this guy for a while, and a few months later, we're on midnight shift. It's the middle of the night, two or three o'clock in the morning. I'm still writing. He sees a kid somewhere off of Lorain Avenue, crawling out of an apartment basement window, and he's carrying a bag of stuff that later turned out to be a couple of six packs of beer. Anyway, he says, "Look, over there on your left. There's a kid crawling out of the basement window, and he's running." And he got the car to a stop. It was a snowy, ice cold night. Everything's slippery as hell. It's all ice. I jump out.

I'm on foot and I'm running. And I can hear my portable radio. He's circling the block, trying to figure out where it is we're going to come out. I went in between buildings after this kid. And I can hear him broadcasting on my portable, and he's panic-stricken. He says, "Doran is out on foot alone. Here's where we're at. She just ran westbound through a parking lot. She's back behind the building."

He speeds around the corner, and he's broadcasting this, as the police car's literally spinning in circles on ice in the middle of the intersection. He's trying to come to a stop so he can come and assist me. Every zone car in the district comes screaming in to see where I'm at. And as they all slide in there sideways on the ice, I come out from behind the building. I got this kid by the back of his shirt and I'm kicking him in the rear-end. And I said, "That's for making the old woman run." I get him to the side of the police car and the policeman I'm working with takes the young man from me. He pats the guy down. He puts him in cuffs and puts him in the back of the car. He turned around and he slapped me on the back so hard he almost slapped me out of my winter boots.

He said, "Good job, Doran." And I said, "Do you remember the first conversation we ever had?" He said, "Yeah." I said, "You need to know that I was kind of hoping that tonight was coming."

DANIEL LENTZ
Patrol Officer, Third District

It was summertime in 1998. I was working day shift. I think I was still on probation. I was in court. In trial. So I'm not really on the streets. But I'm dressed in my full gear and I have my radio. They had dismissed me for lunch. I'm kind of cursing under my breath and thinking, I don't want to be in court all day. I had just recently got on the job and I'd like to do something. So I went down and had a coffee at the coffee place at the bottom of the Justice Center. I turned my portable radio on. And right when I turned it on, they had broadcast about a male jumper on the Lorain-Carnegie Bridge.

And I said, well, I'm right downtown, I might as well go swing by and see what's going on. I drove over to the Veterans Bridge, the Detroit-Superior Bridge. I see some cars that are stopped, and in the middle of the bridge are some pants, some clothes. I look up on the steel girders and there's a guy, buck naked, about to do a swan dive off the bridge.

I'm confused because nobody's around. I look across the river to the next bridge over, the Lorain-Carnegie, and I see about 30 lights, there're ambulances, police cars and a fire truck. They were on the wrong bridge.

I grabbed my portable [radio], looking at a naked guy on the girder, saying, "Wrong bridge, everyone. I'm actually here. I'm at court, but I'm standing here talking to a guy that's about ready to jump."

I went to his pants and found his wallet. I found out his name. He had a tuberculosis card in his wallet and pictures of his kids with their names. So I started talking to him. He didn't really want to talk about personal things, but at that point I believe I established some type of bond with him. But when everybody responded, they shoved me out of the way. They brought in all the bigwigs. Even the Crisis Intervention Team showed up. They started talking to him and the guy almost jumped.

They said, "Get that kid back in here." When they did that, I started talking to him, and I informed my supervisor that I told him that I would be willing to go get him. I told him to sit down and I'd be willing to come get him.

Well, in the course of talking to him, he sat down. And I said, "Does that mean what I think it means?" He said, "Sure." Then my supervisor started to argue about sending me out. Eventually, they told me that I could go up if I wanted to but they were advising me against it. They had a cherry picker there from the fire department. I climbed up in the cherry picker. I wound up climbing out and I crawled on the girders down the middle of the bridge. I got a couple arm-lengths from the guy and sat down.

I started kicking my legs just the way he was doing it. We talked for 45 minutes. I told him if he jumped, I might as well jump, too, because I have problems just like him. We came down.

HOWARD WISE
Police Photographer

You learned everything. My first partners were Joe Miller and Eddie Hyson. We'd haul drunks to jail, injured people to the hospital, lots of auto accidents and babies. We delivered babies.

The first one we get was an OB call with the address. We go and the lady was on the floor of the car and the baby is coming out. This is on Prospect Avenue at afternoon rush hour. I worked that day with Emil Zane, and we were both young.

The baby was my turn to deliver. I thought I did everything right but I got a little nervous about cutting the cord. So we called for assistance. Another car pulled up, a couple coppers. They said, "Howie, we're not sure. We're not positive. I don't want to make a mistake." So they called for another car and two old coppers pulled up. They said, "Yeah, you got it right. Cut it." So we cut it and the baby survived. Everything was good. I got a certificate in my scrapbook upstairs for that.

PETE MIRAGLIOTTA
Patrol Officer, Fourth District

I worked with two old timers, two really great guys. Usually for the first three to five days, you ride three men in a car. You're like the third man in a car. Well, we get some kind of bullshit dispute on Warner Road. I had grown up in and around Warner Road off and on so I was pretty hip on the neighborhood. It was some white kid. He had a motorcycle and a dispute, whatever.

So I'm just standing there with my thumb up my ass so I decided to look at the bike. And in my mind, I'm trying to think, "Where did they tell me the VIN number is on the bike?" So I'm looking around and looking around and this long-haired asshole comes off the porch. This guy starts telling me to quit eyeballing his fucking bike. Well, I don't want to get into a problem with this jerk. I don't want to disrespect my two partners, my training officers, by not acting like I'm not watching them, but they're doing some neighbor mediation shit. It's my third day on the job. I'm not even really—this is, seriously, 72 hours of me being on the police department. So he says, "Why are you eyeballing my bike, man?" I'm like, "I'm just looking at it." He's like, "Why? Do you think you want to tow it?" I'm like, "Look, I don't want to have no problems with you."

So they're kind of looking over their shoulder like, "Why is he getting into it with this guy?" This guy was just starting and he just wouldn't stop. Finally I said, "Look, why don't you just shut the fuck up and go back on your porch. I'm not here to hassle you, talk to you, or anything. Actually, I'm just here to observe." He says, "Oh, you're a fucking rookie. You stupid motherfucker."

So I decided he was acting in a disorderly fashion. I brought him to the ground, handcuffed him and put him in the car. My partners look at me and go, "What are you doing?" I said, "I'm making a fucking arrest." "For what?" "I don't know. I'll figure it out when I get to the station." They thought that was really cool, but they wouldn't let me know. So now I'm sitting there in the backseat with the guy and he's kicking the backseat, he's handcuffed. And I don't even have no clue. I know it's disorderly conduct because I asked him to quit.

So we're going to the double doors of the Fourth District and we get to the bullpen area, and they just leave me. And then nobody comes to the booking window. So I have no clue what to do. I mean, I've gone through it at the academy, but I have no fucking clue. Meanwhile, they're telling everybody, "This kid doesn't take any shit. He just popped this guy and threw him down and handcuffed him." So they think I'm great . . . But meanwhile, they're all walking by the booking window. And I've never seen the Fourth District booking window. The guys working the booking window are looking at me as if they're saying, "You stupid fuck. You're in so much trouble. Why did you arrest this guy?"

They let me stew like that for about 40 minutes. I'm sweating profusely. I walk in there and the sergeant comes up. He goes, "What do you have here? What's up?" I walked up to one of my guys and I said, "Jerry, do I have to book this guy?" He said, "Well, you're a fucking cop. You arrested him. Now book him." And he walks away. The same thing with my other partners.

This actually goes on for almost an hour and a half. Finally I said, "Fuck this." I took the keys, opened the booking cell up, threw him against the fucking window and I said, "Somebody want to fucking book this guy?" And they just cracked up laughing. It was something stupid, but they were all just laughing at me. They say, "Well, what are you going to book him for?" "For being fucking stupid. For aggravating me. If it's not a law to piss off a fucking Sicilian, then I'm making it a law to piss off a Sicilian. Disorderly conduct."

JAMES MCMANUS
Patrol Officer, Impound Unit

My first day on the job, I was working nights. We didn't get an opportunity to have a roll call because they had a shooting incident that happened in the projects on West 150th Street. They needed all cars available out of roll call. So we all left our roll call, jumped in the car. I didn't know what I was doing, just following the field training officer that I was assigned to.

We zoomed up there. We made it there in about—well, let me say we made it there real fast. When we pulled up, there was a van that was blocking both the incoming and outgoing traffic. It had been shot up. You could see the bullet holes in there as we pulled up.

It was just a shooting. We didn't know who was the shooter, who was the victim, or what. It was just a shooting that came over the radio. We got out of the car. When I approached the van, and as I passed it, I saw the bullet holes and blood on the windshield, on the car door windows, and someone opened the door. There was no body in there, but you could just see blood trails going in different directions.

Someone said it was a Jamaican shootout or it was drugs or what have you. After we searched the neighborhood, we couldn't find a victim, a suspect or anything. No one ever came forward. We didn't find out who did what.

That was the first few minutes on the job.

DANIEL LENTZ
Patrol Officer, Third District

I was out of the academy less than a month and I get run over by a car. It was January, and it was a multi-car accident on I-77 southbound, close to the East 55th Street exit. It was night and it was freezing. That was what caused the problem.

There was a little dip in the road and it was icy. We had several of our own cars there. Lights were on and flares thrown on the roadway. They were diverting traffic. We start walking toward the accident and I'm focusing my attention on all the broken-up cars and all the damage and looking at the policemen and the civilians on the side of the roadway. They're taking information reports and I heard a girl's voice, kind of like a whimper and crying.

I looked over the median and there's a girl on the opposite side hiding and crying. She was probably in one of the original cars in the accident, but the cars kept slamming into her and she bailed out of her car and jumped over the median.

I reached over and convinced her to grab me. She put her arms around my neck and I picked her up and started carrying her. I remember somebody screaming, and when I turned I could see headlights. I threw the girl out of the way and attempted to dive and the car may have hit my legs and spun me around like a helicopter.

I wound up laying next to the vehicle. I'm in my raincoat and I felt a terribly hot feeling. It was the car radiator that was spraying antifreeze on me. I get up, I grab the girl and we hobbled over to the other side of the roadway. We went to the hospital. I had an impinged shoulder and knee damage. I eventually had knee surgery for it.

CHESTER TORBINSKI

Lieutenant, Accident Investigation Unit

I'm appointed September, October. Come November, about the middle of November, the sergeant says to me, "You're off for the next six days."

I said, "What, am I laid off?" You never heard of a policeman getting laid off in those days. He said, "No, that's your vacation." I said, "Six days?" He said, "Yeah, you get a day-and-a-half for each month."

I said, "Well, I only worked two months. That's only three days." He said, "No, for the rest of the year. You worked from November, December, that's six days." I said, "Oh, all right."

I came home and I'm telling my mother that I'm going to be off next week. She said, "Why?" I said, "Vacation." She said, "Vacation. You only worked two months. How can you get a vacation?" She said, "What did they do, fire you? Did you do something wrong? Aren't you fit for the job or what?" I couldn't convince her. Then I was off that whole week. I was off one more day.

So when I was going to work, I put my suit on. She said, "Where are you going?" I said, "I'm going to work. Vacation's over." That's when she said, "I can't believe it. You work two months. You got six days off." I said, "Good job, huh?"

TAMI TONNE

Sergeant, Narcotics

My partner and I got a complaint of dope selling in Lincoln Park, off West 14th Street in Tremont. So we pull up and [the suspect] runs. I'm driving across the park, between the trees. We chase him and he runs across West 11th Street. He's going behind the church there. I went the other way because I thought the kid was going to come back around. Sure enough, that's what he did. I don't see where my partner is, but the kid is coming right at me so I grab and tackle him. I put him right down on the ground. He was crawling and I refused to let him go. My partner arrives and handcuffs the guy. He had seen the whole thing and he said to me,

"I can't believe you tackled him. I can't believe the way you were driving. You're a really good driver." So I impressed him. After that, he didn't mind working with me.

WILLIAM DANIEL GALLAGHER
Patrol Officer, Third District (retired)

I got out May 10, 1956 and my first assignment was the First District. I don't know about population, but it was the largest of the districts in geographical terms.

Burglary, stick-ups every now and then, little gang stuff among kids. But basically, I sort of got a kick out of working in the First District.

My first day on the job, we had about four one-man cars. We had four other two-man cars, two mobile patrols, two wagons, an accident car, a detective, and a juvenile car. And we handled everything. Now they have 50 cars, almost, in the district, but they still can't handle it. They really don't want you to be a policeman [now]; they want you to be a social worker. But that's the nature of the beast.

When I came on the job, I was broken in by World War II vets. And they were sharp. I worked with terrific policemen. They knew their job. They knew how to deal with the public. They were good street policemen, too. I don't think they were people who over-reacted, but they had a lot of patience. I don't think policemen nowadays have that patience. But maybe I'm wrong . . .

You see both sides to people, the good side and the bad side, a lot of times. But like I said, I worked with good people. They broke us in and all that. In fact, I think the first day I went out on the car, I worked with my uncle, and we had a tornado. I worked 16-, 20-some hours the first night out on the job, out on the street. We had a bad storm. It did a lot of damage. I was at West 86th Street and Denison Avenue and I was driving. The storm hit, and I had my feet on the brake and the car was rocking. And stairs just flew right by us, porch stairs. It just missed us. It did a lot of damage on the West Side. But that was my first night on the job.

TOM ARUNSKI
Patrol Officer, Third District (retired)

After four days, we went on midnights to eight in the morning. I was working with George Walter, a nice guy and a nice policeman. We get this call at East 55th Street and Broadway, upstairs apartment, male disturbing with gun.

We pull up to the building. There was a hobby store and right next to the hobby store a stairwell. This hallway was narrow enough that both of us couldn't walk up it together. So I'm going up and George is behind me. The guy we were looking for was banging on apartment doors. He thought his girlfriend lived there, but she lived two blocks away. But he was so drunk and crazed on drugs that he didn't know what he was doing.

He's banging on the doors, yelling and screaming, raising all kinds of hell. When he saw us, he said, "You need more than two guys to take me." George said, "Come on, we'll just escort him downstairs and take him to jail."

The guy pulled away from George, reached in his back pocket and pulled out a gun. I drew my gun and I got it in his ear and I'm

---

I'm pulling the hammer back. I'm thinking, "I'm killing this guy and I got four days on the job. This is nuts."

---

pulling the hammer back. I'm thinking, "I'm killing this guy and I got four days on the job. This is nuts. We're not supposed to be doing this."

Thank God George knocked the gun out of the guy's hand and yelled, "Don't kill him! Don't kill him! Don't kill him!" I put my gun in the air and kicked him down the steps. As he's rolling down the steps, he's saying, "When I get up, I'm gonna kick your ass." I said, "Hell, you're not getting up off the ground. You better stay there when I get there." The guy's name was —— I'll never forget him, and I've forgotten a lot of things over the years. He was my first arrest.

JIM GNEW
Patrol Officer, SWAT

My first assignment was the Fourth District. If I had to do it all over again, I'd go to the Fourth. Back when I came on the job, it was a dumping ground. If you screwed up, you went to the Fourth. So all the garbage in the department, they sent out to the Fourth.

But I learned one thing out there. I probably learned teamwork in the Fourth better than anything else, because when you were out there, nobody messed with you. These guys all stuck together. If somebody kicked your ass, there were 10 other guys to kick that guy's ass. So it was a very close-knit group. And, for whatever a lot of guys did to get thrown out there, they were good police officers. They did their work. They were such a good group of guys that when I'd see guys from my academy class, maybe run into them at court or something, and they'd say, "Sorry you got sent to the Fourth," I'd say, "I had a ball!"

You learned what police work was all about. You'd have two or three or four shootings every day. There was never a quiet time. You'd do 10 or 12 or 15 or 20 runs. They weren't illegally parked car runs. Usually, it was shootings or stuff like that.

I even delivered three babies. Unfortunately, one of them was in Rawlings Junior High School, just off East 79th Street. She was around 13 or 14. I remember my partner telling me, "Kid, when you go there and it don't look like the baby's ready to get born, tie their legs and throw them in the car and get them to the hospital as fast as you can."

It was funny because when I first got to the Fourth, we didn't have any police uniforms because the city didn't have the money at the time to buy them. The Fourth was tucked away on East 131st Street and Union Avenue. I was late the first day I showed up because I couldn't believe it was a police station. I kept driving back and forth in front of it and saying, "There's no way that's a police station." All the cars were parked in back. You couldn't see them from the front. When I finally walked in, they said, "Well, kid, first day on the job and already you're late." Back then you didn't say shit. You just kept your mouth shut. Because if you opened your mouth to those guys, they'd smack the shit out of you. They told rookies what to do and they said we were there to shut up and learn and we didn't know anything until they said we knew it. That's the way it was.

Over the years it changed quite a bit, but the thing that I see, I don't know, I just don't think that's there's the togetherness anymore. It's like everybody's an individual. Before, we'd actually depend on each other to get things done. If you'd go to a gun run or something like that, you weren't going up there by yourself. You didn't have to ask for help, there were always cars there. And we still managed to have our fun. For me, it's always been work hard and play hard. I like it that way.

WILLIAM TELL
Commander, Sixth District (retired)
For my first assignment, I was third man ride-along. You rode along with the old-timers and they showed you the ropes. We were at 116th Street and Kinsman Road. And we got a call for a car theft in progress on a nearby street. We responded and we walked up on this Ford. I didn't see anybody in the car. But the two guys I was with saw the guy. They drew their guns and started yelling at the guy to come out. There was a guy, he had put his hand up inside of the dashboard trying to hot wire the car and his hand was stuck in there. They were screaming, "Come out! Come out! Come out!" And they pulled the door open and the guy pulled his hand out. He had a hand full of blood and everything because it was stuck in the car. Actually, the car caught this guy.

* * *

The first week on the job, I was shot at on Drexmore Road and Van Aken Boulevard, right on the Cleveland–Shaker Heights line, of all places.

We were on a two-man ride-along, with an old-timer whose name I'm not going to tell you. Old Timer never wanted to take his shotgun out of the car. He didn't want to just get the job done. The other rookie was William Stanley, who wound up being deputy chief of police. They generally put two veterans and one rookie. But this night, they gave us two rookies with just Old Timer. We

---

Old Timer turned us into the boss and said, "I never want to go with these guys again. They're wild kids."

---

got a call about shots fired. A man tried to steal a car. So Old Timer responded to the area. When we got there, we saw the guy run behind an apartment building. When the thief saw us, he turned around and he fired a gun at us. So we went to shoot at him and we heard Old Timer screaming, "Get back in the car! Get back in the car! Get back in the car!" So we ran and got in the car, thinking that Old Timer was going toward the guy who shot at us. Old Timer went the other way and took us back to the police station and turned us into the boss and said, "I never want to go with these guys again. They're wild kids."

We didn't do anything wrong; Old Timer just didn't want to get involved with it that night. He took us back to the police station and Old Timer never worked on a police car after that. Old Timer worked in the station from then on. He was always an office man from then on. We kind of prided ourselves with ending his career.

MIKE FRICK
Sergeant, Second District (retired)

In 1970, my rookie year, I was working the upper end of the First

District, the Puritas Avenue and Rocky River Drive area. We got a call of an accident on the Brookpark Road Bridge, going into Fairview Park. We were at Grayton Road and Puritas Avenue. We get there and there's a car on fire, a head-on collision on the south side of the bridge. There was a green Pontiac Tempest coming eastbound over the bridge. There was a Thunderbird containing two guys going westbound.

The guys in the Thunderbird were more than likely intoxicated because it was 2:30, 3 o'clock in the morning. They struck the Tempest head-on and drove it back 100 feet. With that, the gas tank in the Thunderbird erupted. The two guys in the front seat died. They were burned to death.

We had just pulled up on the scene and the fire department hadn't even gotten there. The guy in the Tempest was still in the car and alive, the dashboard was right up to his chest and the steering wheel was over his shoulder. He was transported to Fairview Hospital where he died.

After the fire department put out the fire, AIU came out to investigate. Photos were taken and measurements, and since we were the first car there we assisted in directing traffic. The coroner's office showed up with their big meat wagon. Me being a rookie, I got the fine job of assisting, helping him remove the bodies.

One guy was slumped forward in the passenger's seat and just all burned up. The other guy was leaning backward with the steering wheel in his chest and he was all burned up. At the time, they had only one guy in the coroner's wagon. I said, "I'll go over there," and he gives me a pair of latex gloves and says, "Okay, we gotta get this body out."

The fire department cut the steering wheel out and the driver was taken out and put in a bag. The passenger, who was smaller than the driver, I think he was cooked more. I reached in and grabbed him and pulled. It came right out of the socket. I'm holding an arm.

It was the first and only time I got sick on the job.

4.

"So my partner and I . . ."

[MEMORABLE CALLS]

KEVIN GRADY
Patrol Officer, Fourth District

In the fall of 1998, my first partner and I were in car 413. We were at East 143rd Street and Milverton Avenue. I was in the middle of a felony drug arrest when we heard a series of gunshots. It sounded like automatic gunfire. It turned out to be almost 40 blocks away, but I got on the radio and advised that I heard 15 or 20 rounds being fired.

A couple minutes later, I heard a call for shots fired into a house. It was around East 102nd Street. The front of the house was riddled with bullet holes. Turns out it was hit by an AK-47 on full automatic. Almost 40 bullet holes in the front of the house. This all happened around 12:30 or 1 o'clock in the morning.

I walked in the house. Immediately to my left was a room filled with a lot of people, mostly policemen. On the bed was a woman. The headboard of her bed faced the front of the house. Most of the bullets went right through her room. An AK-47 is a powerful round. Some of them went through the house and through the garage out back. The woman had been killed, shot to death while she was sleeping. Now remember, I only had about a year on the job at this time. The rounds had mutilated her; both of her eyes, for example, were gone.

But what shocked me was the way the family was handling it. Everyone was sitting at the dining room table, smoking cigarettes and drinking coffee. It was as if nothing happened, or it happened so often it wasn't worth getting upset about. The mother was killed because one of the kids at the table hadn't paid a drug debt. The victim was 47 years old and worked in a health care facility.

I remember a rookie, a black female rookie, was there and watching this scene and she became very upset because not one member of the family showed any concern for the mother. The rookie said, "How the hell can they just sit there acting like this? Their poor mother just got shot." I said, "Welcome to the Fourth."

ROBERT CERBA
Lieutenant, Fraternal Order of Police

One shift, I was working with my normal partner, Glen Jason. Winter of 1991. We received a call to assist EMS with a dead body in the Garden Valley Projects. We get down there and walk into the apartment. There's a male between the bed and the wall, obviously dead, with a bunch of clothing covering him. Like, he had a pile of clothing on him and he fell off and it fell on him. Something didn't look right.

I pulled a couple pieces off and there was blood all over his face. And there was a broomstick handle sticking out from under the clothes and everything else. I think you can figure where this is going. Needless to say, Homicide gets out there, we get our Scientific Investigation Unit out there. They start taking pictures of him after they took the clothing off. Here this guy had been shot and then stabbed in the neck. The knife was still sticking out of his neck. He had been beaten in the face with a baseball bat so bad that we didn't know he was shot until he went to the coroner's office. He had a broomstick shoved up his rear end. Somebody wanted this guy dead pretty bad.

For the next couple of days, we canvassed the whole area down there. I have what I call snitches out there. I was telling everyone, "If you get any information, call me." Nobody wants to say anything. Everybody was quiet. It gets around the projects who done what. It gets around. But nobody was telling us anything. About a week later, me and my other partner, who was on the car, Steve Warshaw—he's a lieutenant now—we were working together and we got a call down on Kinsman and Minnie. That's a little side street that runs across from the drive-in. We got a call to go down there for males robbing people. They gave us a description. We go down there, and right at Kinsman and Minnie there was a little check cashing place, between 75th and 79th. We come pulling up and there were people matching that description right there.

We come flying up, jump out, grab them, and I threw them on the wall. Right then, the third guy comes around the corner. My partner spots him and he takes off after him. I don't want my partner running through the Projects. As soon as he cut the corner of the building, I didn't know where he went. I didn't know if he went across the street in the Projects or where he was going. So I pat my guys down real quick. They don't have any guns on them. I'm worried about my partner. I don't know if the guy he's chasing has a gun. I don't want my partner to get in a shootout and not have me there.

I didn't have time to throw the cuffs on these two guys and throw them in the back of the car, so I just pushed off of them and jumped in the car and took off after my partner. So my partner winds up catching him. We throw him in the back of the car and go back over to the parking lot and call for help. We find the guy's gun laying on the ground. So we're protecting that. The other cars come pulling up. Here comes the other two idiots walking back through the parking lot. "Hold them!" So we have all three.

We find three separate victims. All of the victims identify all three of the guys. One of the victims tells us, "I think that car is theirs because they were in it." We [go] over and start searching the car and find another gun. So we've got three robberies. We've got three males arrested, two guns confiscated.

So we go back to the district . . . We had three separate reports. We had three separate victims. We had to mark and tag the guns and all those things. I'm sitting there and the phone rings in my office. It's one of my snitches. He says, "One of the guys that you arrested is the guy that killed the guy in Garden Valley."

So we're there already in overtime. Six o'clock in the morning comes. The office man from Homicide usually got in at six. About quarter after six, I call Homicide. I get the office man. "Hey, listen, the homicide from last week, the guy with the broomstick shoved up his rear end? We made an arrest last night, some robberies, and one of my snitches called and said one of the guys that got arrested was the guy that did it."

I told him we had the guns. I'm sitting there, finishing up my reports, marking the guns. I hear, "Cerba!" I said, "I'm back in the office. What do you need?" "Homicide just called. They're on the way up right now for those guns." I said, "Okay. I got them back here. I'm finishing up."

Homicide comes out. They grabbed all three of the males. They grabbed the two guns and took them downtown. They test-fired the guns. One of them turned out to be a positive. They took the guys in the office and started sweating them for which one it was, and broke the guy who did it in about a half an hour.

Here it turned out the killer and the victim were cellmates in prison. The victim got out about two months prior. And the other one got released about a week before. Since they were cellmates in prison, he wanted to get some jail pussy. And when the guy refused, he killed him. And that's why the broomstick was shoved up the guy's rear end. It was because he wouldn't give him a piece of ass.

JOE ROGERS
Captain, Fifth District (retired)

At the Lakeview riots, I was with Lieutenant Tad Woodruff, who had too much guts. We're standing at our car, five of us, watching a couple hundred looters smash the windows of stores and loot them. Lieutenant. Woodruff says, "Let's get the tear gas and clear out that store."

So we get the tear gas grenades out of the trunk of the car, march over, and when he said to throw, we threw. The grenades landed, made three little pops with three little puffs, about as big as a puff on a cigarette. The looters were watching and they started laughing. We started laughing, too. Then the lieutenant said, "Let's go, men. We've done our duty." Well, it turns out those grenades were from World War II.

MIKE O'MALLEY
Detective, Homicide Unit (retired)

Homicide certainly isn't glamorous. I always tell people who ask, "This is not television. In 42 minutes, we can't solve a murder and get a conviction."

Homicide certainly isn't glamorous. I always tell people who ask, "This is not television. In 42 minutes, we can't solve a murder and get a conviction."

People don't die nice. People don't get killed nice. I try not to bring it home with me, but with an investigation, you're always thinking. A lot of people don't understand, but even when we're home, we get paged with calls from other policemen, other agencies.

We worked the murder of officer Wayne Leon in June of 2000. Investigating the murder of a police officer is especially difficult. You're dealing with a case where you know the individual who's been killed and some of the family and extended family.

You have to be guarded in your emotions because you have to be pragmatic. You know you have a very serious responsibility. In three months or six months, you're going to court with the suspect and you don't want the case thrown out because of something you did that was inappropriate.

I've had a very good career. I've been fortunate. I'm often asked, "Why don't you want to get promoted?" I never wanted to get promoted. I enjoy what I do. And I couldn't do what I do if I got promoted.

LEE ASHCROFT
Patrol Officer, Scientific Investigations Unit (retired)

Auto theft was big then. And actually, that evolved into the traditional spyglass [surveillance] detail on the top of the buildings. But crime really picked up downtown. The type of crime where Mary Smith is at her desk on the fourth floor of the Leader Building and she goes out for lunch and comes back and her purse is missing.

The boosting people started getting brave and started going into the office. And that's when security started coming into effect downtown, more so than it was before. The downtown area was changing drastically. The department stores—Sterling Davis, Taylor's, Halle's—they were all moving out. They had nothing but May's and Higbee's left. So the downtown scene was changing drastically. There was less emphasis on crime.

Actually, crime was moving out, too—out to the Fourth District, and out to the Sixth District. Eventually, the Fifth District, where I had gone to the academy, eventually they were overtaken by urban renewal, which ended up at the Cleveland Clinic, and crimes were driven even further out into the Sixth District.

Then there was no such thing as a burglar or robber or a pickpocket. Crime started integrating into one class. One day, they might try picking pockets; the next day, a crime of opportunity, breaking into a window of a jewelry store if nobody's around or something like that.

But so-called experts, no.

We used to see some beautiful safe jobs. Pick-n-Pay had their safe burglarized one night. I think they got $5,000. And to see the magnificent job they did of burning into that safe; how they scored it off and measured. They knew where the tumbler mechanism was. They burned in perfectly. Most pseudo-safe crackers, as soon as they go in, they knock the pins off the door, maybe knock a couple off and expect the door to fall off. It doesn't work that way. But there were safe men out there that were great. But as they grew older, when you start arresting suspects after an investigation, some of these suspects, you can give them the best safe tools in the world and they wouldn't know how to use them. So the era of the so-called excellent criminal went down the tubes.

JAMES MCMANUS
Patrol, Impound Unit

We were sitting at the light and the light had just turned green for us to go, and this guy zoomed past. He ran the light. He was in a four-door Oldsmobile, a 1978. And he was probably doing about 60 or 70 miles an hour. If he would've hit us, he probably would have done some damage. And as we chased him for a while, he managed to make it to an on-ramp over by I-90.

We were chasing him on the highway and he was swerving in and out of traffic. And we finally got to the point where we got close enough and he pulled over and we called in where we were and said what had happened. We didn't know what his problem was. There were two people—him [the driver], and the passenger. So my job was to watch the passenger, and my partner was monitoring his activity.

And as we approached the car, the first thing I saw in the backseat were cases of beer. You could not see his backseat, there were so many cases of beer. And as I made it to the passenger door—it was a four-door vehicle—and the passenger on that side was a female, and she had her hand over her face, shaking her head, like she was disgusted with the driver.

So I asked her to step out, and she got out of the car. She was explaining to me that the driver was her boyfriend and he was drinking. My partner opened the driver's door, and she asked him to get out of the car. He got out and the first words that came out of his mouth were, "What the fuck do you want, bitch?"

So, she said, "Do you know you ran a light back on Denison and you have been speeding and recklessly operating your vehicle?" He goes on and says, "Fuck you, bitch. I don't care what you say." He balled up his fists and he puts them up as if he was getting ready to box her. So, at that point, I came around the front of the vehicle and approached him from behind. And as I approached him, I explained to him to calm down and he turned around and looked at me and the first thing he said to me was, "Oh, a nigger." He startled me because I had never been called that on the job by anyone. That's the first time I had encountered that.

So it threw me off for a moment, and at that moment he swung at me. As he swung at me, I saw his fist coming at me and I moved my head and he missed. And as he missed, he staggered out into the roadway, and cars were coming by and they nearly hit him. By then he was probably in the middle lane and he was just standing there holding his fists up, dancing around like he was Muhammad Ali or something.

He said, "I'm going to beat both of your asses," and all of this stuff. Now I had become a little angry, and I'm sitting there monitoring the traffic and it appeared that he was going to be hit. At that time, honestly speaking, I really didn't care.

My partner looked at me and she said, "James, we've got to get this man out of the street before he kills himself." I had thoughts of letting him kill himself. We both walked out there and by that time he had danced his way back toward the car.

I told him, "Sir, I need you to calm down." And he said, "What? Didn't I tell you, no nigger tells me what to do?" And so he put his hands up and he swung and he missed. He kind of staggered back out into traffic. So my partner told me, "We need to take control of this guy." As he swung again, he missed, and I punched him in his mid-section. He bent over and he screamed. We both rammed him into the front end of his car. As we handcuffed him, he was screaming a bunch of obscenities to her and myself.

We were walking him to the car and she stopped and said, "Well, you write him out some tickets for the speeding and running the light . . . I'm going to go do an inventory of the car and speak to the young lady."

I walked him back toward the zone car, and when we got to the zone car I opened the back door and I told him, "Sir, you need to get in the car." He said, "How many times do I have to tell you, nigger, I'm not going to do what you tell me to do." So I said, "Sir, I'm not going to ask you again. Get in the car." And he said, "Fuck you! What are you going to do if I don't?" At that point, I'm thinking he needs to get in the car. He won't get in the car. I'm pissed. I regret that he slammed his head into the car. Quite hard.

He sat down and I went to close the door and he stuck his leg out. So I said to him, at that point, "Move your leg, sir, so I can close the door." He wouldn't move his leg. I asked him again. He wouldn't move it. I asked him again, and he wouldn't move it.

So I just revved the door back and I shut the door and it accidentally hit his calf. Then he started screaming and yelling. Then he moved his leg and the door closed. I got in and got my ticket book—I don't remember how many tickets were in the book at that time, but I had never used it—but I think it was over 15. I wrote his name on every one of them and filled them out with all kinds of offenses after that. But each ticket that I had had his name on it.

While I'm writing out his tickets, he started shouting some more obscenities and screaming real loud. My partner came back and she asked him, "Did you drink all those cases of beer in the back?" And he said, "I don't know, probably." And she said, "Sir, there's 12 cases there. You drank all 12?" He said, "Probably, during the course of the day." She said, "Well, that's special."

He asked her, "Can I ask you a question?" She said, "Yeah. What is it?" He said, "Well, how long have you been fuckin' that nigger over there?" At that point, she nudged me with her elbow and she said, "Oh, we've been fucking for about a year now." And he said, "Ahhhhhh. Ahhhhhh. That's what's wrong with this country now."

She looked at me and said, "Oh, yeah, and he's got a real big dick, too." He said, "Ahhhhhh. I don't want to hear this." And she said, "Oh, and we're probably really going to do it after we book you." And he said, "Ahhhhhh. I hate you. You fucking cunt."

BOB TONNE
Detective, Robbery (retired)

My best arrest was off duty. I caught three bank robbers just before they went in the bank. That was 1978. I got letters of commendation from the FBI and everything. I had a day off and I had to go to court. So I took the detective car. I was going to go to court. I thought, "I'm going to stop at that bank and show some pictures to some people to see if they can identify them."

I come up to Public Square. Right at Public Square, the car in front of me—I memorize license numbers; that was my forte. I memorized 150 of them—and this car in front of me, I said, "Geez, there's that license number."

The bank robber gets out of his car, I recognized him. He walks in front. He had two accomplices, a woman and a man. They stayed in the car. I jumped out of the car; put my gun on them. She dove underneath the front seat. He put his hands up. I got them both out of the car, and another policeman came walking by. I said, "Hold these people. I'm going after the other guy inside."

So I started walking down Public Square. I picked up an officer, a detective who was reading the paper. There's the bank robber, standing outside of the bank. I grabbed him, turned him around, put the cuffs on him, and nobody knew what the heck happened. He had the stick-up note in his hand yet. So that convicted all three of them. In fact, they gave it to the FBI and they put six bank robberies on them. I got a letter from the director of the FBI. I just got lucky. I was at the right spot at the right time.

DENNIS WONDRAK
Patrol Officer, Fourth District

I'd always heard rumors about the Fourth District. I heard it was a busy district. And it's nowhere as busy as it used to be. A lot of people will ask me, "Why don't you go to the suburbs and be a police officer? Why work in the ghetto?" Well, the bottom line is I can work in the ghetto. I like it. I like the adrenaline rush. I'd be bored in the suburbs. I can do the job, so I will.

That's doesn't mean I don't get scared. When Officer Schmidt was shot, I went to see him in the hospital. His head was huge. No

---

Good thing I don't think about that when I'm putting my shoes on. Otherwise, I'd never leave the house.

---

disrespect, but it was the size of a pumpkin. And I told my partner, "That's the pain of reality. Good thing I don't think about that when I'm putting my shoes on. Otherwise, I'd never leave the house."

I deal with two types of people. Good people having a bad day and bad people having a normal day.

DANIEL RUTT
Patrol Officer, First District

We got a call to go over to a street off of Lorain Avenue. First it came down as the ex-husband trying to set fire to a house. Then it came down as shots fired. When the original car arrived on scene, they observed a female laying in the grass, and the suspect was in a red van. They gave the license number. We were at the top of the street and they said he was heading westbound on Lorain.

There was a sergeant; she was a little bit ahead of us. She spotted the car a few blocks away and was trying to pull it over and it wouldn't stop. We went to assist her. She got in front of the car to slow it down. When it stopped, we went up and apprehended him.

What had happened was, his wife had just won some lawsuit against him. They were divorced. He went to try and set her house on fire, and when he couldn't set the house on fire, she came out and started yelling at him. He went over to his van, got a gun, shot and killed her. There were children around the house. They were standing around her.

So, back at the car, he was reaching down next to his seat and the weapon was right next to his seat. But when we got him downtown, he didn't realize what he had done. He was so drunk. He was a little, old Irish guy. And he was so drunk he didn't realize what he did. This guy had to be in his 60s. He kept saying that the bitch got what she deserved. And, I can't remember exactly what the comment was, but the idea was, he thought that he had just hurt her real bad. He didn't think he killed her. They were married 20 years.

* * *

All criminals are pretty stupid. One guy kind of sticks out in my mind. He was up on Rocky River Drive and Puritas Road at the Drug Mart. He went in to purchase some milk or something, probably for his family, and he dropped a bag of marijuana on the floor. The security guard picked it up and asked him if it was his when he was walking outside. The kid turned around and said, "Yeah, that's mine." So they started fighting inside over the bag of marijuana. The police were called and they took him to jail for possession of marijuana. He was 19. Stupid! They were fighting over, probably, a $5 or $10 bag of marijuana.

MIKE FRICK
Sergeant, Second District (retired)
We get a call about a house being broken into. It was one of the coldest winters in Cleveland history. It's on East 79th Street just north of Kinsman. We pull up and a couple guys bail out of the house and take off. We started chasing them. We never caught them, so we go into the house.

The house is freezing cold and we heard some movement in the bathroom. We open up the bathroom door and here's this little old lady sitting with an electric heater going, trying to keep warm.

We talked and found out she had no furnace. This house had to be 150 years old. Just a couple days before this we received an assignment to go to a house in the same area where these two old people, a brother and a sister, were found in bed froze to death. They had no heat in the house, either.

My partner and I decided she couldn't live under these circumstances, so my partner went up to a restaurant on Broadway and got her dinner and hot tea. I got on a neighbor's phone and called all these agencies. Well, it was midnight and I wasn't getting any answers so I called the American Red Cross. They told me they couldn't assist because she wasn't a fire victim.

I told [them], "What do I gotta do? Burn the house down before you're gonna come out and help this little old lady?" And the answer was, "Well, I'm sorry."

So I called a reporter I knew from the *Plain Dealer* and asked him if he wanted a story. I explained to him about this old lady who was so cold and I couldn't get a hold of any agency, how I got a hold of the Red Cross and they refused. He was there in no time. The next thing I knew, he made a phone call, Red Cross was there and they put her up like she was a victim of a fire. They put her up at the Lake Erie Motel.

But that's not the end of the story. I had an aunt who worked for the Red Cross, and after reading the newspaper article she called me and said, "You don't know what you did. That article. Everybody down here is getting their ass kicked because they didn't help."

Well, there was a police supervisor who was very close to the Cleveland chapter of the Red Cross, and because I embarrassed an organization they took me off the streets and stuck me in jail. I was the jailer in the Fourth District. For about three or four weeks I had the shit jobs in the Fourth. I wasn't allowed to go out on the streets until my aunt intervened with the head muckety-muck from the Red Cross, who got to the supervisor. I did something good, but I embarrassed an organization. Well, what can you do?

WILLIAM DANIEL GALLAGHER
Patrol Officer, Third District (retired)

We had a captain, Bill Zimmerman, that worked out of the First District—hell of a guy. Anyway, I'm working a one-man car. I'm up by Jefferson Park. I had just been talking to him. He was out riding around. And we get a shooting at around West 116th Street, just north of Lorain Avenue. One guy killed another guy. Anyway, when we got on the scene, here the victim's laying dead on the tree lawn, people all around. I was the first guy there.

Zimmerman came up second. They said that the guy was inside with the gun. So Zimmerman and I go in. We were in the kitchen. I can remember the kitchen was very small, and the guy had the gun. I was shitting in my pants. I mean, I didn't know what to do. I was young. I was scared, really. And Zimmerman's talking to him and he reached, "Give me that gun, you son of a bitch."

I'll never forget that. He was a hell of a guy.

I didn't want to get stuck making the report. It wasn't my zone, you know. So, anyway, a broadcast came in that there was a Royal Castle on West 160th Street and Lorain Avenue. It was being robbed and I volunteered to take the Royal Castle robbery, but Zimmerman said, "Get back here. You're going to handle the homicide." Which I only had to make the report and all. The next day, I came into work and Captain Zimmerman said, "Come on in my office. Put a tie on, we'll have our picture taken," and the newspaper photographers took our picture.

DENNIS SWEENEY
Detective, First District

We've had some great arrests. And it's more of a team effort than an individual effort. The best one probably—me and Bob Wolf and Jerry Zarlenga and our boss, Sergeant Dennis Hurrelbrink—we had a guy who was robbing. They called him the Silver Gun Bandit. He was robbing stores, gas stations. He hit, probably, four or five counties. They said he did over fifty armed robberies. And we were on him for probably two or three months before we caught him. But we ended up catching him at West 30th Street and Clark Avenue.

It was the fall of 1996. We got a tip at the time from Brian Heffernan who was a sergeant in the Second District. He worked Vice at the time. He told us that this guy might be copping heroin down near West 30th Street and Clark Avenue. So I ran down there in an unmarked car. And Wolf and Zarlenga were coming down to meet me because I had gotten in before they did. And I was going to do surveillance.

The car that he was using in these robberies, it was a yellow—I don't remember what type it was, a Dodge or Aries—one of those Aries K cars. We got a call about a week earlier that he was on West 85th Street, painting it with rollers, white. And by the time we got there, the car was gone, but there was an outline of a car. That's the truth.

So the first thing I noticed when I pulled up at West 30th Street and Clark Avenue at this big grocery store; I see this white Aries, and it's flat white. Well, no one was around. I had a motorcycle leather on and a bandana. I looked like someone from the neighborhood. So I walked up to the car, and sure enough, you could tell that it had been painted with a roller.

I had a picture of this guy. I know Wolf and Zarlenga had to be real close. They're coming from the First District. They're flying down there. One of the employees came out for a cigarette, and I said, "Hey, I'm looking for this guy. I think he's inside." As I'm showing the kid the picture, the asshole walks right up in front of me. The only reason he didn't look at me, probably, was because of the way I was dressed. Also, when he turned, I heard wheels turning. But I didn't know at the time, that was Wolf and Zarlenga.

So I grabbed this guy by the back of the leather. I stuck my gun in his ear. As I turned around, Wolf was already out of the car and has the guy's arms together and has them up in the air. Wolf's a strong kid. He just picked him up like that. Zarlenga handcuffed him. When Wolf put the guy down, we pulled a chrome-plated .357 out of his pants.

We took him down to the district and we kept him going with coffee and a lot of sugar, and he confessed to more than 20 armed robberies in Cleveland, and said he was willing to talk to the other communities. I think it was Geauga and Lorain counties. He did it all over. He asked me to apologize to the women who he had put a gun in their face. That's what he asked me. I said I would if I had the opportunity. I'd let them know he was sorry.

I asked him afterward if he had the opportunity, would he have shot us. He said, "Yeah." He said he would've, but he never had the opportunity so it didn't matter. As a matter of fact, when we had him up at the district, he actually calmed down. He wasn't that bad. He told us he had a $250, $300 dollar-a-day drug habit. He was doing heroin, coke, crack, whatever—whatever he could get his hands on. He was moving around, west side, east side. That's why we couldn't track him down.

KYLE STOUGES
Patrol Officer, Third District

I met my wife, a Cleveland paramedic, at a bar fight. It was at West 117th Street and Lorain Avenue. Guns involved, bats, broken beer bottles, all kinds of stuff. It was fall of 2000. Night shift. It was a big fight. There must have been 15 zone cars there, all the cars in the district. And EMS starts getting dispatched. Three ambulances arrived because you had people with their faces cut up, broken arms from the bats, among other things.

I met my wife, a Cleveland paramedic, at a bar fight.

It was funny. I was sitting there taking information. I had a woman with a blood-soaked T-shirt on her face, trying to hold the blood back on a cut she sustained on her forehead and cheek from a bottle. I'm taking the information and she's sitting on the curb.

My sergeant, a fantastic lady, walks up and says, "Well, why don't you ask her out?" And I said, "Sarg, she's sitting here bleeding." And she said, "No, dummy. The paramedic over there." I said, "Oh, what, was I staring at her? Is it that obvious?" Kerry McClure. As soon as I saw her, I fell in love. And that's not like me.

JIM GNEW
Patrol Officer, SWAT

On the upper end of Kinsman Road, right around East 123rd Street, the bars were out of control. Drugs, shootings, beatings every day, and especially on the weekends. On weekends there was so much illegal parking there, it was ridiculous. We used to go up there all the time, but one night I remember in particular.

These bars all had one o'clock licenses. They all had bars on the front of their doors. After they locked the inner door, they would shut the bars, put the lock on it, and leave. This one night we're there and the street was infested with cars and it was already past one o'clock. Roger [Dennerell] had probably forty tow trucks with us and we're going up Kinsman. All the bars had their doors open and the bars open, too. We took the bars, the grate, and shut them. We stuck locks on them so no one could get out and we towed every car on the street. Every single car. When the last car was gone, we undid the grates and let everybody come out. They were bitching up a storm. The problems started disappearing.

ALAN CIELEC
Patrol Officer, First District (retired)

During the summer of 1982, a female officer was filling in for my partner. For some reason, we both looked in the rear of the parking lot at Wendy's on Lorain. It's two o'clock in the morning. There's a house in the back parking lot and there's a window and a light on. There's a guy in the parking lot. We pull in and I turn off my lights. We get out of the car and see he's bald. He's dressed in women's clothes.

I said, "Sir, can I talk to you?" He jumps in his station wagon and takes off. He's westbound on Lorain and we're giving chase. He went down Lorain, down into MetroParks and somehow on to I-480. There are five police cars chasing this guy and I'm the fourth car because I'm not going that fast.

As we're flying along I-480, the guy is getting undressed and throwing his clothes out the window. Blouse, bra, nylons. He threw his wig out and it got caught around my windshield wipers.

As we're flying along I-480, the guy is getting undressed and throwing his clothes out the window.

So I turned the wipers on and this wig is going back and forth. And my partner's laughing her ass off. So I had to reach out and grab the wig to pull it off. I broke the wiper, too.

The guy gets off at Great Northern Boulevard and we chase him down Lorain again and then down a side street. And all of a sudden, he pulls over. They threw him against the car to search him, but there's nothing to search. He has nothing on except panties. So they cuff him and I said, "I'll order the tow." And Danny Crawford, who was the first police car there, looked at all of us and said, "Who wants coffee and who wants tea?"

I said, "Where are we gonna get a cup of coffee or tea at 2:30 in the morning on a residential street?" And he said, "I know the guy who lives in that house right there. I'm gonna go wake his ass up." And he did. And the guy made coffee and tea. Danny was a tea drinker, like me. There were nine of us there, plus the guy in the panties.

I said to Danny, "Beats me why he pulled over," and everyone started laughing except me and my partner. One of them said, "Don't you know why? We shot his goddam gas tank out. He ran out of gas." I don't know if it was lucky shots or what, but they did it. And I don't know what car did it or what policeman and I don't want to know. All I know is I didn't do it.

* * *

Tim Leahy was my partner in 1980. One day in the summer, we're chasing somebody and the guy bails out. Tim Leahy is the passenger. I'm driving. As Tim jumped out—he got one leg out—a dog runs up and bites him on the ass. We never did catch the guy.

JAMES MCMANUS
Patrol Officer, Impound Unit

Me and my partner had one of those days where it was dead. We couldn't even find anybody who was parked illegally. Nobody even littered that day. I don't know what it was. We got a call to just go check out a house. The neighbors were calling that there was something odd going on. This was off of Detroit Avenue, near Lakewood.

As we got closer, there were two people on the porch and they were walking down the steps as we got there. They were two undercover detectives. They said "We were already in the area and we heard it on the radio, so we thought we'd check it out, but since you guys are here, you actually got the call, so you can check it out." They didn't get a chance to knock on the door or anything. So they left.

My partner knocked on the door with no response the first time. So, he knocked again, but he knocked aggressively this time. He knocked real hard, and as he did, the door swung open. He looked at me and I kind of shrugged my shoulders. So he just looked in and he started shouting, "Hello, hello. Is anybody here?"

And no one responded so he walked in and I followed him. We looked around and the house was—you couldn't see from the door to the end of—it was like a group home or something. There was a great big stairwell and a big living room as soon as you walk in with a long corridor leading to the back of the house. The first thing he did was he said he was going to go up the steps to see if anybody was home. He told me to check out the downstairs. I walked around. It was in the evening, going into getting dark, maybe around seven o'clock, on a fall night. And as I walked in the back of the house, it had gotten dark, so you needed to put the lights on to see around the house. So, I opened this one door and it led to the basement. I tried to put the lights on and no lights would come on, so it was real spooky around there. I just yelled to see if anyone was there, "Hello, hello." No one responded.

And at that moment, my partner yelled to me to come upstairs. So I walked up the steps. When you got up the steps, it was another long corridor and there were just doors all the way down the corridor, the hallway, just multiple doors. So, we walked, knocking and opening the doors, and he's saying, "Hello, hello."

We get to the next door and he's saying, "Hello, hello." So he just pushed them open and shouted, "Hello." I was behind him and I would just walk in the room and look around as he opened them. So when he got to this one particular door, he knocked and he said, "Hello." I heard the door kind of squeak open and just at that instant, I heard him scream, "Oh, fuck! Oh shit!" So I ran toward where he was and he dove on the ground. And he told me to get down. He was like, "Watch out, Jimmy, the guy must have a machine gun or something."

So at that point, I'm totally oblivious to what he's talking about because I didn't see what was in the room. So I crawled to where he was and then I could see a body laying on the ground. It was laying face first and there was a woman in the bed with covers on. She appeared to still be alive. She looked like she was having a nice rest or what have you.

As my partner got up, I got up. In the instant that we got up, you could see blood marks coming through the sheets from where the woman had been shot. She had finally started bleeding. There were 11 holes that blood was trickling from. Her eyes were closed. We got on the radio and we called for assistance. We checked other rooms, this time more forcefully, then we went back to the bedroom. We wanted to guard the room until help got there and monitor it because it was a crime scene.

As we were standing there, my partner decided to touch the male who was laying on the ground. Technically, he probably shouldn't have, but he touched the man. He rolled the man over, and as he rolled the man over, the man had a gun in his hand and a box of ammunition in his hand and a great big bullet hole in his forehead.

Apparently, what had happened, he came and shot the woman with his .38 he had, all six rounds, then he shot her five more times, and the last round, he shot himself in the head. As he fell, the box of ammunition he had fell all over the floor. When we realized what happened, I felt bad for the lady because it looked like he had just done it a few minutes before we got there because the sheets were drenched, but they weren't like that when we first walked into the room. He had just done it a few moments before we got there.

And I felt bad for her and wished that we could've gotten there a little sooner. As we came down the steps and opened the door, the house was now surrounded by police cars. There were news media people out there. I guess they must've been listening to the radio. I came out and there were people sticking microphones in my face, asking me what I saw and what had happened. I was still feeling bad for the lady. I really was speechless.

And another police car pulled up with a gentleman in the back seat. He got out and he had a cast on him. He was the person that was at home when the suspect came in the door. He was in the bedroom watching television. He said that he saw this man walk in the door with the gun in his hand and the ammunition and he was loading the gun up as we walked in the door. He said, when he first saw him he knew him because he was married to this lady. He had just gotten out of the workhouse for domestic violence. He saw the guy. He spoke his name and the guy didn't pay attention to him.

Then he said at that moment, he saw the guy loading up the

gun and walking up the steps. He said he jumped out the window. He had a cast that covered his leg from the tip of his toe to his knee and he jumped out the window and hobbled to the corner to get away from the house because he saw the guy going up the steps with the gun. She was in her sleep when he shot her. By all accounts she didn't even know that he did it. She never woke up or anything.

JOE ROGERS
Captain, Fifth District (retired)

When I was a sergeant in the Sixth District, we got a warrant to serve. The charge was first-degree murder. Well, we're not supposed to get those; the detectives are. When my guys asked me what we were supposed to do with it, I should have said, "Send it back," but I didn't. I said, "Let's go serve it."

We get to this apartment and kick the door in. We race in but the only person there was a woman and she was in the bathtub. We asked if the guy we were looking for was there and she said, "Hell no, and what are you doing in here?" We left and one of my guys said, "Now what do we do?" and I said, "Fill out a damaged property report for her door and send the warrant back to the detective bureau where it belongs."

ROY RICH
Captain, Fraternal Order of Police

It was Christmas Eve day, early in the morning. My partner, Mike Spiro, and I had just finished taking a mentally ill woman to Charity Hospital, which was outside the Fifth District. The Fifth ended at East 55th Street, and Charity was East 22nd Street. It was a snowing, cold, nasty night. We were just leaving Charity, talking about getting something to eat. We were downtown and we could run over and grab a gyro at Best Steakhouse. We were talking about that and a call came over the radio: "Any car in the area, male is threatening his family with a shotgun." The address was just off East 55th Street.

The car that answered the call was at the other end of the district. It had two officers who had about a year each on the job. From our point of view, they were rookies. I had nine years then and Mike had five. So I looked at Mike and said, "What do you think?" He said, "Oh, man, I don't want to kill anyone on Christmas Eve," and

---

So I looked at Mike and said, "What do you think?" He said, "Oh, man, I don't want to kill anyone on Christmas Eve."

I said, "All right, then we're not going to go," and he said, "All right, you're right," and he picked up the radio and said, "Five-twelve. We'll be responding from Charity. We're relatively close."

Mike steps on the gas and he was about the best wheelman I ever knew. We pull around the corner on East 55th Street. As we get close to the address, we shut off our lights. We see a young lady standing outside at the curb, waving to us. She was wearing only a pair of gym shorts and a tee shirt. At that point, we knew it wasn't good. Nobody stands out in the snow unless there's some real bad situation going on. She pointed to the house and said, "My stepfather, he's crazy. He's scaring everybody with that shotgun. He's just inside the door. The whole family's on the couch."

We called back and said, "Tell back-up to shut their sirens down before they get here. The house is lit up and we're going to check it out." We walked up on the porch. The screen door was closed, but the inside door was ajar a couple of inches. The door had three panels of glass. I could see his face through one panel and the second panel down you could see his arms, and in the third panel you could see him holding the shotgun. Actually, it was a rifle. He was pointing it at a family sitting on a couch. He was screaming at them, sounded intoxicated.

Mike looked at me I looked at him. I had our shotgun in my

hand. I've already got it pointed through the center glass, thinking I'll hit him in the chest if I need to. Mike looks at me and we look at that door and he opens the screen door very quietly. The guy's still screaming at his family, doesn't even see that we're there.

Mike gives me a one-two-three, lifts his leg and kicks the door in. The guy turns toward the door. It hits him in the face then we shove the door and it knocks him to the floor. His hands are on the rifle, but his finger's not on the trigger. I come in with the shotgun above him. I've got it pointed right at his nose, four inches away. I'm yelling, "Drop the gun, drop the gun, drop the gun!"

What I'm watching for in my peripheral vision is the muzzle of the rifle. If the muzzle moves toward the family at that point or toward me, I'm going to take him out. Mike is right next to me with his handgun. What I recall most vividly was his eyes. I didn't see hate. I saw confusion. He threw the gun away.

We get him up, cuff him and as we're dragging him to the car, he's saying, "Aw, man, gimme a break."

I said, "You got a break. You're still breathing."

PETE MIRAGLIOTTA
Patrol Officer, Fourth District

In the early '80s, me and Dave Kwiatkowski were on night shift. We get a call, early Sunday morning, "Shots fired. Male with a gun. Screaming in the background." You've got to remember, you've been up all night; it's Saturday night. All you really want to do is go home.

So we go basically plowing into this place off Buckeye Road. It was kind of like a half-ass cheat spot, where they stayed up all night partying and stuff. We go busting in the house, through the front door. As sure as shit, as soon as I open up the front door you hear, *bang*. So the adrenaline kicks in, and you're like, "Okay, let's go."

We go up these ratty stairs, I hit that door, and there's kind of like a mirror. And I see this guy—*boom*—it looks like he's putting a coup d'etat—into the body on the ground. I come around the corner, and as soon as he sees me, he drops the gun. This guy can't be more than 20 years old. I put him against the wall and handcuff him.

We get an ambulance, and unfortunately, she passed away, so it's a homicide. So we call Homicide. We bring the shooter to the Fourth and put him in the jail cell. They used to bring these shitty lunches for prisoners. It was your responsibility that if you put a prisoner in, if it was morning, they had baloney sandwiches or a cup of soup, a piece of fruit and this cold coffee. You gave it to them when you put him in the cell.

So, I give him this shit. And the guy's being relatively nice. And as I walked back there, he keeps going, "Man officer, this is a good apple. This is a good apple. Man, if I had another apple, I'd be set." He said, "Officer, do you think you could get me another apple? If I had me another apple, I'd be set."

I'm like, "What?" So I said, "Dave, come on back here." I said, "What do you need?" He said, "Officer, if I had me another apple, that apple was awful good, I'd be set." I'm like, "How old are you?" He said, "Twenty-some years old." I said, "You know, you'll probably go to jail for life." He said, "I know." I said, "And that's all you want right now is an apple?" He said, "Yeah. If I had me another apple, I'd be set." So we went down there and got him another apple.

JEFF STANCZYK
Patrol Officer, Third District

There was this shoe store broken into on West 25th Street in the early '80s. They only put one shoe in the box so you couldn't steal the shoes. So, a couple of coppers were in there. We went to assist. One copper throws a shoe at the other one. Pretty soon there's a shoe fight going on. The owner finally comes. He goes, "It's a good thing we got all this on tape." We're looking at this thing going, "What a bunch of jackasses. Picking up this guy's shoes." We're supposed to be there securing the scene, and we're throwing shoes. And he was cool about it. So, the next day you get up, and you go down West 25th, and you see people walking around with one new shoe and one old shoe.

WILLIAM TELL
Commander, Sixth District (retired)

The smartest criminal was a car thief by the name of Cotton. These guys were the best car thieves that I've ever seen in my life. This was 1970 to 1980. It was a family. They would steal cars and remove serial numbers off of them. Or they would go and buy burned out cars, go and steal your car—an identical car and they would take the car and flip the bodies. They would take the burned portion of the car, throw it away and then put the part of your car on that burned—a body flip.

I dreamed about a case once. And I solved it. I was working on the case that I had—and it was a very intricate case, because we had an Oldsmobile that was stolen from Randall Mall, and it was supposedly burned up, but we arrested a guy driving the car and it had never been burned. And so I went to sleep and I dreamed that Cotton did it. Then in my dream, I solved the case, and I got up and wrote it down on a piece of paper.

How did I catch him? He didn't change the glove box lock. I

> Policemen don't catch criminals
> because we're good. We catch
> criminals because they screw up.

had the glove box taken out of the car and taken to Cleveland Key. And they duplicated the box with the numbers on it and I was able to open the glove box and trace that box back to the owner. The owner came with his keys and opened his glove box. So that's how we got him.

I dreamed about it because it was on my mind. As a police officer, you get cases, work them, and your most difficult cases, you dream about them. You just sit there and dream and, "That's what it is!" That's how you solve them. You don't solve crimes because you're some rocket scientist. You solve crimes because people are stupid or you solve by luck. You stumble upon them. Policemen don't catch criminals because we're good. We catch criminals because they screw up.

MARGARET DORAN

Patrol Officer, Mounted Unit

One of my last stops at basic patrol was at the Fifth District, on midnight shift. And my captain out there is now one of the supervisors in the Bureau of Traffic, shift captain—Bruce Henke.

And the captain called me into his office one day and he said, "Doran, I was talking to the district commander about you." I looked at him and I said, "So, Captain, what did I do this time?" He said, "No. I told the commander that Doran is like a breath of fresh air blowing through here. We forgot this job was supposed to be fun." He said, "And I've been looking at your work. You're pretty good at what you do. I read your police reports. I've heard of your exploits out there. I told the commander that I wish we could find a way to keep her here." I said, "Holy shit, incentive to stay on midnights in the Fifth District as a one-officer car. Well, perhaps you could double my salary. Because, if you can't do that, I think I hear a horse calling me."

HOWARD WISE

Police Photographer

The fire department had a fire in a flophouse and they had to kick in the door. It was at East 55th Street and Woodland. They found a dead woman laying on the bed and called the police because it was a homicide. I'd say she was only dead a few hours. Not that long, because the rigor hadn't set in yet.

The woman had been stabbed, probably, 50 times. There were knives, forks sticking in her, gas pipe sticking in her. The guy who killed her drew on the wall in her blood, "I killed her because she treated me like a dog." I got pictures of that. It was her boyfriend. They knew who did it.

You know, when I moved to Florida—my wife and I moved to Florida—the Naples Police Department borrowed my whole collection of crime scene pictures. They wanted to borrow them. They said they'd never see anything like that in Naples, Florida, what they would see in Cleveland. They had them for a couple weeks and they brought them back.

You have to leave the blood and guts at the job. You can't take it with you. You've got to forget about it.

ALAN CIELEC
Patrol Officer, First District (retired)

One hot, summer night in 1986 we got a call for an intox driver involved in an accident at West 73rd Street and Denison Avenue. We go over and there are already auxiliary police directing traffic. We threw the intox driver in the back seat and while we're getting the information, a car comes through the red light almost hits one of the auxiliary policemen. He scraped him.

So we jump out, grab the driver of this car, who turns out to be intox, too, and throw him in the back seat. We tell the auxiliary guys where to have the cars towed and we head up to Lorain and start westbound with the two drunks in the back seat.

We're stopped at a light when a citizen pulls up and asks us where he can get gas. Now, the guy just drove by a 24-hour So-hio station, so we're thinking he's either drunk or lost. My partner says, "Yeah, go to that gas station right there. It doesn't look like it's open, but it is. He's probably sleeping in the back room, so you might have to beat on the door to wake him up. But sometimes he forgets to shut the pumps off, so try to pump first before you wake him up." We pull off to the side to watch. He pulls up to a pump, takes the cap off his tank, tries to get a hose off the pump and he's really tearing at it. Finally, he puts the pump back and goes to pound on the door. While he's beating on the door, the alarm goes off and the lights are blinking off and on. The two drunks in the back seat said, "Man, that guy's worse than us. You better take him in."

So we pull in, grab him, cuff him and throw him in the back. We left a note for the station manager not to have the guy's car towed, that he'd be back tomorrow to get it. Now we have three drunks in the back seat and the first two guys are laughing their asses off.

When we get back to the district, the lieutenant says, "There're zone cars out there than can't bring in three drunks a week. Only you guys could bring in three drunks at one time."

GARY EUGENE KANE
Sergeant, Strike Force, Sixth District

Nobody outran me. Not in those days. My first two years I was on, nobody outran me, period. Because I was fast. That's all there is to it. We had a stop one day on Franklin Avenue some place. And a guy takes off running. He had at least a 30- or 40-foot head start on me to begin with. This is in the middle of the afternoon in the summertime.

He takes off. I don't even know why we were chasing him, or why I went after this guy. He looked at me before he started running. He looked at me, and he thought he's just going to run and he's going to get away. Your eyes just meet for that second, and he's like, "Yeah, I can leave him behind." My mind is, like, "Nope. There's no way." So the chase is on.

He's running. I'm running. We're going through yards. Everybody's out, looking. It's the middle of the summertime. There's a field with a four-foot-high fence there. Going through the yards, he's opened up his lead but I'm not quitting. So he's probably about 20 yards ahead of me at this point. And we're going through this field. And there's about a four-foot fence. He slowed down to hurdle the fence. He's slowing down to get up on the fence and go over it. And I was looking at the fence from where I'm at and I'm saying, "I can jump that." Then part of my mind is saying, "You *can't* jump that. You better slow down so you can get over this fence." By this time—and I'm running flat out—it became do or die, because I'm too close now to slow down and be able to stop. And I jumped and I just made it over. I came right to the top of the fence and push off.

And it seemed like the whole neighborhood was, like, "Wooo." Then I'm right over because I haven't lost any time on the fence. He looked back and saw me and just stopped and laid in the street. Everybody's around and everybody's looking and they're just, like, "Woooo."

You know, after a point, you stop running, when you get old enough.

PAUL BURGIO
Patrol Officer, Fourth District

The first time I worked with Dave Hutchison we were in one-man cars. He was on a missing persons report and I heard him call for his supervisor. Me being nosy, I thought I'd slide by. It's a quiet day, a beautiful June day and it's quiet. It's a nice house on Martin Luther King, Jr. Boulevard. There's a young lady in her early 20s who's reporting her mother missing. She's upset because she hasn't heard from her mother in three days and she's never gone a day in her life without talking to her mother.

So we end up at the home of her mother's boyfriend's mother, where the missing woman was supposed to be house-sitting. Dave wants to go in the house because the woman has been missing for three days and there was definitely a smell of something dead to this house. The supervisor comes and says, "Aw, that's a chitlin smell. That's a dirty house and chitlins. Make the report and get out of here." And he took off.

I said to Hutch, "Well, you know he didn't order you to leave. He just said to make the report and leave. And part of the report is, you've got to talk to the neighbors."

So we go knocking on the neighbor's door and the woman said, "A couple nights ago, I heard a loud argument, but I went to bed and didn't think twice about it. And I know the owner's out of town and I haven't seen her son over there. He was supposed to be watching the house." She had a number for a daughter and we asked her to call and see if she could bring a key. She did.

We explained what was going on and she looked kind of leery. She opened the door and let us in. We walked in this living room and it's just destroyed. There's a thick marble dining room table just busted up. There's a large-screen TV just ripped to hell. And it looked as though somebody had taken a paintbrush and splattered red paint over the walls and ceilings. There's a thick, dark red trail from the middle of the dining room all the way through the living room, up the stairs.

Dave looked and said, "Oh, dude, we gotta call the boss." I said, "We don't have anything yet. We got a dirty house." So we draw our guns and say, "Police, police," identifying ourselves. The stairs went up to a landing and turned. Dave gets to the landing and stops cold. And I'm thinking he's got somebody, so I kind of inch my way up there.

On the second floor landing and all through the hallway, there are messages written in blood. "Hon, I'm sorry. Baby, forgive me. Only God can judge me." In blood all over the house. It was right out of a horror movie. Not just little writing. I'm talking big letters. So we start checking the rooms.

The rooms are lived in, but they're not filthy. The bathroom was spotless, spotless and scrubbed. And there's one bedroom at the end of the hallway that's locked from the inside and the doorknobs are broken off. I looked at Hutch and he said, "We gotta call the boss. We gotta call the boss." I said, "Hey, man, we don't have anything yet. When we get something we'll call the boss."

I looked at him and said, "In for a penny, in for a pound," and kicked the door in. There's a dead woman on the floor. And a naked man dead on the bed. I said, "Okay, now we've got something. Don't touch anything. Let's get the hell out of here." We went back downstairs and called for a supervisor.

I said, "I need you to respond back here at MLK." He starts screaming into the radio, "I ordered you to get out of there. You get out of there." I didn't say anything and then I lost my temper.

I pushed the emergency button and cut him off and I said, "I got two dead bodies, an apparent murder-suicide. Are you coming up here or not?"

There was dead silence. I'm thinking, "Oh, shit, I just yelled at a boss. I just screamed at a boss over the air." So I waited about 10 more seconds and I said, "Do you copy?" Now I'm a little meek again. He said, "I copy. I'm on it."

He rolled up, got out of the car and said, "Good detective work, guys. Excellent job. Way to follow your instincts." We saved his ass. Had we left the house, the old lady would have come back and found her son and his girlfriend dead. The girlfriend had two wounds. One was made with a large carving knife through a pair

---

What killed her was a Phillips screwdriver to the heart.

---

of denim pants in the groin area. What killed her was a Phillips screwdriver to the heart. After killing her and dragging her body upstairs, he slashed his wrists, wrote the messages on the wall and then laid down and died.

SHAWN KNIERIEM
Patrol Officer, Canine Unit

I had not been on the job very long and one summer night two males kidnapped and raped a woman in my district. After finishing with her, they threw her out of the car and sped off. They were going at such a high rate of speed that when they tried to make a right turn, they became airborne, struck a tree and their station wagon split apart. Both suspects were ejected and one was killed outright. The other was taken to a nearby hospital.

My partner and I were holding down the scene at the vehicle when I received further instructions. It seems when the injured suspect was ejected from said vehicle, he became separated from some of this parts. So I was told to try and locate this suspect's genitals. Diligently searching with my Maglite, I remember thinking, "Well, 0200 hours on a hot summer morning and where am I? On Dick Patrol. I'm sure a rat has already made off with it and I'm positive his balls have bounced down the street and into the sewer." I did not locate anything.

ROBERT CERBA
Lieutenant, Fraternal Order of Police

We pull out on Kinsman Road and we're heading eastbound from the district. I had just written down the serial number of the shotgun and put it back in the rack. My partner says, "Bob, look out your window." A car went by us doing 50 miles per hour and no lights on. It was dark. By the time we catch up to it, we're close to Martin Luther King Boulevard. We called in, "441 radio. We're going to be making a traffic stop on this vehicle. We're over at 116 and Kinsman."

The guy pulled into what was a Shell gas station, which is now gone. We get out of the car and the driver starts getting out. Now, normally, if I'm the one that's going to be encountering first, I tell them to stay in the car. I don't want them being out of the car. My partner was driving. He was the one that was going to encounter. I let him do what he feels comfortable with.

So we walk up. They're older guys. I'd say, probably late-30s, early 40s. This was back when I was in my 20s. He was dressed fairly nice. My partner asked him for his driver's license. He pulled out his wallet and he started digging for it. I told my partner that I was going to take a look at the temporary tag that was on the car to make sure it wasn't altered. We hadn't gotten anything back from radio. And the common thing to do was to take some Wite-Out and change the [date] on the temporary tag. I walked up. I no sooner get to the car than I hear my partner yelling for the guy to put his hands up. My partner had tried to pat him down and the guy's moving all over the place.

I go running over there and the guy's just standing there, and he's got his hands down at his side, up under the hem of his jacket. I remember distinctly that he was left-handed. He was facing me. I said, "What do you have in your hand," and I started reaching and he came up with a gun. It was a .38. I quickly grabbed the gun around the cylinder, over the top, because if he did get a shot off, I wanted it to only be one shot. And as long as I was holding onto that cylinder tight, the mechanical advantage was that he was not going to be able to shoot another round.

Unfortunately, where the gun was aiming would've taken out my family jewels. So I started yanking up, figuring, let me get it up to my chest because I've got my vest on. And if the gun goes off, I'd rather get hit in the vest than somewhere where I have no protection. Well, the guy was trying to bring the gun up to me. And the combination of me yanking up and him trying to bring it up, the gun comes up and caught me in the lip. I've got the gun up here and he's trying to force it down, and I'm trying to hold it up.

I hit him in the head with my flashlight as hard as I could. I momentarily stunned him, yanked the gun out of his hand, threw my flashlight and the gun on the ground, and I basically pile-drove him. I take him to the ground. We fought for quite a while before we subdued him. All I could say was, "I should've shot you."

But unfortunately I couldn't [have]. I could have smacked that gun down and gotten my gun out and shot him. But my partner was right behind him. The only thing in the human body that's going to stop that bullet from going all the way through is thick bone, and if I miss it, there's a good chance that that bullet's going to go all the way through this guy. Our .38 revolvers, at the time, were great for shooting holes in targets, but they also have a bad habit of going into a body and right out of it. That's not what you want. You want the bullet to stay in. There's less chance of innocent people getting hit. So I knew in that split second that he came up with that gun that I couldn't shoot him because my partner was right behind him.

You sort of get a bad reputation if you shoot the bad guy and your partner with one bullet. You might not find anybody that wants to work with you. Well, that's some of the stuff that goes into this business that we have to make in a split second. You have to be aware of your surroundings. Even if my partner were able to jump out of the way, on the direct line from where I was, people were at the window. So if he wasn't there and I would've fired, that

---

You sort of get a bad reputation if you shoot the bad guy and your partner with one bullet. You might not find anybody that wants to work with you.

---

bullet still could've went through and hit one of the civilians at the window. I don't want to do that. If I have to shoot a bad guy, I want it to be a bad guy alone. Not somebody else. I don't want a tragedy.

My lip was laid open and I had to stop at the hospital and get five stitches. One of the charges against this guy was felonious assault of a police officer. But he told the investigators that I hit myself with my flashlight. The investigator asked me, "Are you sure you didn't hit yourself with your flashlight?" I pulled out the flashlight, and set it on the desk. It weighed about three or four pounds with the batteries in it and everything. I looked at the flashlight and I looked at him and said, "Do you think I hit myself in the mouth with that flashlight and didn't lose a couple of teeth or at least loosen them? All I got was a split lip?" He said, "I see your point." And that's all I wound up with, was a split lip.

BOB RAINEY & ELMER WALLING
Patrol Officers, Statement Unit (retired)

RAINEY: All I remember is it was in the month of January, and it took the whole month of January.

WALLING: We worked on this—a statutory rape case.

RAINEY: We were the only two who could take this thing. The

captain said, "You and you." It was Captain Haufschild. Haufschild was in charge of the Detective Bureau. I don't remember Haufschild's first name. But I never called him by his first name; it was always Captain.

WALLING: If you can just picture a young girl. Now, I don't know if this is true, but I remember her having pigtails. And she would come into the Statement Unit, and the boy, her boyfriend. But he was like a little mouse. She led him. Her name was Judy.

She was a little girl. She looked like a little baby to me. Anyway, she could take her finger and run it down the phone book and tell you every name on there. But she was always making her comments about you. Like, she would say to me, "You're so ugly." Then she'd say, "You're the dumbest person I've ever met." Somebody would walk into the room and she would say, "What are you looking at?" And she used to sit down and fold her one leg up underneath her like that and fold her other leg. She would be smart, like you wanted to choke her. But she had this kid, this boyfriend, would take her down 65th and Detroit. And she would know the addresses of every building. She knew how many steps she went up. She knew the numbers of the apartments. She would tell you. She would get guys and have sex with them. She would tell the detectives. They would go out and arrest them. They would put them in a lineup. She'd go upstairs and pick them out. She would come down and tell us what happened. Now, either Rainey would take her one time or I would have her. You would have the boyfriend back and forth and they would verify who this is.

WALLING: Statutory rape. There was never any money involved. She, like I told you—she went into the fire station on Harvard and Lee and she started having sex with firemen. The bell rang. They all left. They went and took care of the fire. They came back and she's still laying there. And they finished having sex with her. The detectives went out there and arrested everybody in the fire station. She had police cadets. I remember she had a police cadet. He had sex with her down on a police boat or something. He is the only one that was indicted and charged and went away or something. And he was fired, because he admitted it. All these other guys would tell you nothing . . .

She went into a Forest City place, I remember, on Harvard or someplace. There was this old guy who was a security guard. And she had sex with him. And they were bringing people into his office—he was a night guard—but he got fired. Now, I remember—he says I'm wrong but I remember—there was a prosecutor involved.

I remember she went into a place where they fix cars. And she told one of the guys in there that she could outlast him. And they went into a room and they were in there for five or six hours. The boyfriend just sat there. Every time, he just waited until she got done and he'd take her someplace else. Now I always thought there were, like, 30 guys. He said there were 300. And they indicted 54, he said. I don't remember that many.

WALLING: The boyfriend did nothing but drive her. And there was nothing in it for him. Not a darn thing. This was his girlfriend and she had to have sex. He took her around for sex. This is what he was doing. And this went on for—I don't know . . . it was constantly, day after day after day. After they'd run out of all these guys. Now during this time, the detectives went and they made her up like a little girl because she was going into the grand jury, in between arresting guys. And they had her made up like a little girl. They fixed her hair up. She was 15 years old. And after they went through all of these guys, they took the boyfriend and took him to the county jail where all of these guys were and they gave him the blanket job and beat the shit out of him, and that was it. She refused to testify. He refused. Everybody walked. After all this!

RAINEY: Three hundred cases and that's as far as they could go because nobody would testify.

WALLING: We were under the impression that she was going to testify. She would go in the lineup and pick out these guys. She would go into the room and tell you what was in each one of these rooms.

RAINEY: Everybody she had sex with, she could tell you the color of the wallpaper in the house, what room was where and every-thing. This girl; just amazing.

WALLING: Yeah. But it was so sad all the people, all the lives she ruined.

ED KOVACIC
Chief (retired)

This guy, Terry,* was on trial for a bombing and during the trial, he leaned over to me and said, "I know about a murder on the West Side." After the trial, I told Terry to tell me about the murder. He said, "Remember the day you stopped John D.* and me in the car?" And I said, yeah. He said, "Well, we had just killed Frankie M.* We killed him and we burned him behind the gas station on West 25th Street. We put him in a 55-gallon barrel, we burned him for three days, then we buried him down in the basement of a house somewhere on the West Side. But I was drunk, I don't know where it is."

Well, all the guys in the Intelligence Unit are laughing at me. They said, "Do you really believe that?" I said, yeah, I do. I'm look-ing at all these houses on the West Side. He said this house had a dirt floor in the basement. It wasn't unusual. I'd go up and knock on the door and ask, "Excuse me, but does your basement have a dirt floor? Can I see it?"

Terry was doing time in the workhouse for witness tampering and he called me and said, "I've got talk to you." It was a snowy night. I got the police car and picked up my partner and we went. On the way, I slid into a car that belonged to a union official. There wasn't much damage and I didn't want to make a report. I want-ed to get to the workhouse. Terry said he knew something about where the body was. So I told the union guy I would pay the dam-age. I thought it would be 50 bucks. It was $300.

We get out there and Terry's sitting there and I'm mad. He says, "You've got to stop my wife. She's shacking up with this guy. He moved in. You tell that mother that I'm going to blow him up as soon as I get out of here." I said, "You called me down here for this?" I ran around the table and I knocked him under a chair. The guard grabs me. If he hadn't grabbed me and pulled me up, I probably would have killed that little son of a bitch. It was just a whole bad night. The driving was treacherous, hitting the union guy's car and then he tells me this.

So finally Terry says, "I remember something." He remembered the house belonged to a plasterer. We go through every plasterer everywhere, union record, everything. But there was this one house that fit and I was pretty convinced that it was the house. It was around West 30th Street.

I took Terry by it and he said, "No, wrong color. No, it's not this house. I told you the house was white. Wrong color. The gate's the same, but this isn't the house." It turns out the guy who owned the house wasn't a plasterer, he was a taper. He was in the taper's union. You know, how they tape drywall, plaster over it and then sand it smooth.

I got Terry out of the workhouse and brought him over to the house. He said, " I told you this isn't the house." And I said, "Wait a minute, Terry. You said it was a white house. Now, you came up the stairs backward and you were drunk, right?" I put my hands over his eyes. I said, "All right, Terry, I'm going to lead you to the front door." I led him to the front door. I pulled my hands away and said, "Terry, what color is this house?" There was a white door and three white windows. He said, "It's a white house. God, Eddie, this is it! This is the house!"

I got a search warrant and we came back and started digging. The house was vacant. We started coming up with old newspapers. People used to bury their garbage down in the basement. I was coming up with bones and everything. I took the bones to [Cuyahoga County Coroner Samuel] Gerber. He looked at them and said, "Chicken bones. Chicken bones. You don't have any human bones." I picked up one bone I had and said, "Is this a bone?" and Gerber said, "It's a piece of wood." [Assistant coroner Dr. Lester] Adelson said, "When did you ever see a piece of wood with marrow in it? Eddie, that's a human bone. I'm not sure, but if I were a betting man, I'd say it came from somewhere along the sternum."

[Cuyahoga County Prosecutor John T.] Corrigan got us a laborer, the son of one of his assistants. So this kid is digging and I'm picking out these bones. I was a sergeant then and had these two detectives standing there. They're saying, "Chicken bones, chicken bones." I said to the kid, "Brian, the only thing that will satisfy these guys is if you pull out a skull." He said, "I've got something now . . . no, it's one of those kids' bowling balls. I can feel it. I've got my fingers on it." He pulled it out and it was a skull missing the lower jaw.

What led to this murder was John D. and some sort of check-cashing scheme. Terry was doing it and Frankie M. was doing it. Frankie wanted more money and John shot him in the gas station. He went upstairs, reloaded the gun, came back down and said, "Here's how a dago eats bullets." And he kept shooting him.

Bill Coyne was the prosecutor then. On the jury was a very dignified black woman. She was a schoolteacher. We were going for the death penalty. When the jury came back, she was crying. Bill said, "Uh-oh, it doesn't look good. She's crying." Then the jury foreman said, "Guilty of murder in the first degree with a recommendation of mercy."

I said to the kid, "Brian, the only thing that will satisfy these guys is if you pull out a skull."

After it was over, Bill and I talked with the jurors and we asked this woman, "When you came in crying, we thought maybe you were crying because you didn't want to go along with the verdict." She said, "Absolutely not. I wanted to fry the son of a bitch and the rest of the dimwits wouldn't do it."

[* *Names changed.*]

* * *

Harry Leisman was in the Marines for 12 years. He had his own pistol team and everything. Early summer of 1963, we went to Toledo [for a competition] and shot there. On the way home, Harry sees some guy on St. Clair who's wanted and he chases him up over the sidewalk and pins him in the doorway with the bumper of his car. Arrests him, puts him in the car, takes him to the Sixth District and busts him. That's the way Harry Leisman was. It was his own private car. Harry could have been chief of police except he had no respect for [suspects' rights] and he drank too much.

Some poor sap had the misfortune of trying to hold up the Malibu Lounge while Harry was in it. It was across the street from the Arena on Euclid. This was the late '60s. I saw pictures of the guy, and the first three shots were in the guy's chest and the last three were in the guy's forehead. You could cover that shot group with your thumb. When I saw Harry, I said, "Hey, what happened? I thought you were a good shot," and he said, "The guy turned [toward me], he had the gun and my first three were while I was running and my second three I was aiming."

Harry shot a guy in the Hough riots. The guy was on top of a pawnshop and was stealing guns. Harry had a carbine and shot the guy off the roof and then shot him several times as he was coming down.

Then Harry got involved in another shooting. He lived around West 54th Street, I think. He was home and somebody came running to his house and told him a friend of Harry's had just been shot on the corner. He said later that as he was running out of the house somebody handed him a fully loaded M-14 [rifle.] He got over to his friend and the guy took a shot at Harry and hit him in the ass. So Harry cut loose with full automatic and one of the bullets ricocheted into an apartment building where it killed a young kid. Harry wound up being charged with manslaughter in the death of the young kid. He went on trial and was acquitted of all charges. It was the tenor of the times.

At that time, you had to have a heck of a case against a policeman to get him convicted of something, especially in light of Harry being wounded. And I think being wounded entered into the jury's deliberations, that he wasn't functioning normally. His story that somebody handed him the gun as he ran out the door, there was no way to dispute that. The story from beginning to end, it never changed. He fired at this guy who was shooting at him and the bullet ricocheted off and killed this kid.

GREG BAEPPLER
Commander, Second District (retired)

It was the only time, including the riots, this call went out over the air: "Any cars in the city, respond to . . ." It was respond to the Polish Women's Hall on Broadway for a biker battle. It was the fall of 1968 or 1969 and Hell's Angels were having a bike show. There was a gym with a stage and inside were a bunch of bikes, show bikes. There were probably 35 or 40 Hell's Angels there and they were under truce. They weren't wearing colors and they weren't armed.

A group called the Breed, from Pennsylvania, New York, and Virginia decided this would be a great time to rally cut the competition because they knew the Hell's Angels were unarmed. They came in force. When the shit finally hit the fan, there were 80 to 100 of them in there. The Breed had just come in and started attacking Hell's Angels. And then the battle started. It ended up, I don't know, maybe five or six people dead.

Talk about things you'll never forget. We responded. It was, "Any car in the city . . ." We flew over there. It was probably around 11 o'clock at night. We were probably the 30th car there. As far as you could see there were police cars and battles going on. The Breeds were coming out. The Breeds got their asses kicked in there. Believe it or not, they had the Hell's Angels outnumbered and the Hell's Angels, for whatever reason, won the battle. They had their knives on them.

I remember getting into the Polish Women's Hall as this thing sort of broke down, and there was a pool of blood—this is hard to comprehend—there were two guys laying there. One Breed was laying there with a gun in his hand. You know the old joke—"He brought a knife to a gunfight." This guy brought a gun to a knife fight and died because of it. I don't know if he ever got a shot off,

---

You know the old joke—"He brought a knife to a gunfight." This guy brought a gun to a knife fight and died because of it.

---

but he's lying with two other people who were expired, in a pool of blood that was no less than 15 feet around. You know, it was thick, coagulated blood. You know the guy's dead. He's bled out. And the amazing thing was, you've got people lying there, you've got people sort of flopping around because they're stabbed badly and there's not one motorcycle tipped over.

5.

"The first time I was shot . . ."

[DEADLY FORCE]

JIM SIMONE
Patrol Officer, Traffic Unit, Second District

I got shot through the head in 1983. It was my day to get shot. My commander had me working the juvenile unit because of an altercation I had with him. I was sitting in my office and I had my radio on and I heard that they were looking for a guy who just did an aggravated robbery—had robbed a woman. Had told the woman his name and told her where he was going. A church on Broadview Road.

I left the office and told the guy I was working with that I was going to give those guys a hand. It was just a few minutes away. I walked through the front door and guys were searching the upper part of the church. I said, "Anybody check the basement yet?" They said no, so I said, let's go downstairs.

We went down the stairs, and I heard something. I wasn't sure what it was. Didn't hear anything else, and I thought maybe it was just my imagination. I looked down the hallway and I could see a desk flipped over in a room at the end of the hallway. Started down and we searched every room down there. Got to the last room. It was a kids' playroom. It was near Thanksgiving and there were cutout turkeys on the walls. The room was sound-proofed because during services they sent kids down there.

In the corner was a little alcove and a doorway just beyond. I stopped and knelt and leaned around the corner and turned the doorknob. The door swung open. The guy on the other side kicked it open, knocked my hand away from the door, stepped down and put the gun on my face. He pushed my head back a half step or two and then he shot me. Shot me through the head and it blew out behind my ear.

Then I heard him shoot two other officers. I laid there for a half-second and I thought, "You motherfucker." I thought for sure he had killed me. I came up off the floor thinking, "I'm not making this trip to hell by myself."

He shot at me again. It went right past my ear. I couldn't see out the side of my eye. My head was already starting to swell. I was

> I thought for sure he had killed me.
> I came up off the floor thinking,
> "I'm not making this trip to hell
> by myself."

squirting blood out both sides of my head. And I [brought up my weapon] in front of me. I pointed it with both hands and I stuck it up just in front and started firing. I saw the shots hit the wall in front of his head.

He was leaning up against the wall shooting at me with two hands and I thought, "Jesus, I missed him!" I emptied the gun and he was standing over me and he was empty, too. I thought I'd better get out and reload.

I crawled into the doorway and reloaded. I remember I dropped six bullets in my hand and I was looking down in my hand and my hand was full of blood. And I sat there for a second and I realized that I probably wasn't going to make it and I backed up to the wall and I could see the doorway. I put my knees up in front of me, held the gun up and waited. I could hear him in the room. And I was thinking, "Fuck, you got me but I got at least one into you."

I was thinking it's 8:30 in the morning and I'm going to die here. Who's going to tell my kids?

I was in Intensive Care for a couple days, and then came home to recuperate. I had some complications, like migraines and some seizures.

My kids used to think it was a great thing to take my badge to school for "Show-and-Tell" because Daddy's job was being a policeman. That day changed their life. Then it became, "Daddy, do you have to back to work? Why don't you do something else?"

ROBERT CERBA
Lieutenant, Fraternal Order of Police

The first time I was shot at was back in early spring of 1990. I was working with Dave Raynard. We were working on, I believe it was the Fourth Platoon at the time, seven at night until three in the morning. On that shift, you're busy from the minute you walk in the door until the minute you leave. But that's what I like. It was brutal, but I'd rather be on a shift that I can stay busy.

We were touring around down in Garden Valley. We found a couple of guys working on a car. As soon as we pulled up, they took off running. The car turned out to be stolen. So we chased them on foot. On the backside of Sidaway Avenue is the RTA track that comes from downtown, on the Windemere line. So I ran down over the hill and I started chasing them. You could hear them running through the brush and everything. You couldn't really see them because it's pretty heavily overgrown down there.

Finally, we lost them. I had run probably a good portion of the way to East 55th Street. So I made my way back. We did our normal thing, which was call for a tow. Because we were sitting back off the road back in a parking lot back there, we turned on our overhead lights, so the tow truck guy could see us. We turned on our overhead lights and we're sitting there. All of a sudden, *boom! Boom! Boom!* And you could hear the pellets flying over the top of the police car and hitting the leaves on the trees.

We're like, "Oh, no!" We shut off the overhead lights, shut off the headlights, slammed it into gear and we go flying out of the parking lot up to Kinsman Road. We turned the corner and I grabbed the shotgun out of the rack.

I jumped out and I ran back in the projects to find the people who were shooting at us. Because down there we had no idea where the shots were coming from. The way the buildings were set up, you get an echo there, so you can't tell where. If you're in a big open area, out in a field, and somebody shoots a gun, you can pretty much tell, okay, it's coming from over in this direction. With the buildings, you can't. It just echoes off everything and you can't tell where it's coming from. So I run back in and we couldn't find anybody.

Here it turns out that a couple of dope boys from a gang called the Survivors, over off of East 105th Street and St. Clair Avenue, had come down to Garden Valley to rob a drug house. And they kicked it in. They had shotguns and a .22 rifle. This is one of those times when the dope dealers actually came up to the police station and said, "We've been robbed." Of course, they didn't say they were dope dealers, and of course they didn't say that they had anything to do with that, even though we knew that that particular row house down there was a drug house.

"No, no. We don't do drugs. We don't know why they came here."

That was the first time I was shot at. In the intervening years, I've been shot at a couple more times. Luckily, every time I've been missed. It gets the blood flowing, that's for sure.

MIKE O'MALLEY
Detective, Homicide Unit (retired)

The first time I was shot at was about 1980. We were looking for a guy for felonious assault and he was hiding in his mother's house on Carnegie Avenue. As he came through a door, he turned on me with a gun. As I started backing out, he pulled the trigger.

God was with me that night. He had a bad primer. He was only about two feet away from me. It's surrealistic. I can still, to this day, count the number of teeth he had in his mouth. His mother slammed the door and then he barricaded himself inside. He started shooting at us; he reloaded and we called SWAT.

After a couple hours, they talked him out. We went to court. The judge put a low bond on him. And about a month later, he did the same thing. When he went to court again, we suggested he be kept in jail. He had a long felony record and serious firepower in the house. Ever see a replica of a Thompson 25? It's semi-automatic and looks like a Thompson submachine gun. It shoots a .45, a pretty powerful weapon. When we arrested him, he also had a couple shotguns and a .357.

ALAN CIELEC
Patrol Officer, First District (retired)

The first day they created the one-man car, I was working the afternoon shift. I was eastbound on Lorain Avenue and traffic's all blocked up. I thought there had to be an accident, so I drove over the sidewalk up to St. Ignatius Church and here it's two drunken hillbillies, one with a chainsaw, the other with a shovel. They had started a fight in the Sohio station and they're chasing each other in the middle of the intersection at West Boulevard and Lorain.

I'm by myself. These two guys don't have a problem with me, they have a problem with each other. But I'm going to have a problem if they don't drop their weapons. So I pulled out my gun.

At that time we had .38s, with six rounds. So I figured if I had to shoot, I only had six rounds to hit both of them. I yelled, but they weren't listening to me. The chainsaw is going, the guy with the shovel is swinging, and all of a sudden, people started laying on their horns.

Finally these guys wonder what's going on, and all of a sudden they see me pointing my gun at them. Luckily, they dropped the chainsaw and the shovel. I arrested both of them.

Do you know what the guy in the Sohio station was worried about? The gas they put in their pickup trucks. And he's asking me who's going to pay for the gasoline. He gave me a hard time over it. If the guy would have been just a little sympathetic to the situation, I would have both trucks towed. But he wasn't, so I told him, "You know what? These two trucks are on private property. I'm gonna have to leave them. And they won't give me their keys." Of course, I had their keys in my pocket, but he didn't know that. So a two-man car hauled the prisoners away and I left with the two trucks still blocking the pumps.

TAMI TONNE
Sergeant, Narcotics

In 1980, Barbara Parker and I were working together. Basic patrol. We got a call for domestic violence that was just a few blocks from the station. A guy was drunk and fighting with his wife. We go to talk to the guy and he says, "Yeah, I beat up my wife," and we say, "Okay, hate to do this but you're going to jail."

He says, "Okay," and we put him in the car, bring him back to the station, and we're at the booking station getting all the information. All the guys in the station are looking at us, and they start poking each other. I look around and say, "What's going on?" We get done booking the guy, put him in his cell and they asked, "How did you guys do that? How did you get that guy to the station?"

They said that every other time, which was at least 10 times, he fought with them. He must have liked us. He was an iron worker. Big muscular guy. I didn't feel we were going to have a problem with the guy, but I thought to myself that if the guy decides to fight Barbara and me, we're going to have a little problem. Barbara Parker was unusually good at conversations. She used to talk with people. She would talk with suspects and they'd say, "Oh, shut up. Whaddya wanna know?"

PAUL BURGIO
Patrol Officer, Fourth District

I was shot on February 23, 1995, eight months after I graduated from the academy. This guy, Howard Doreman, I'll never forget the name. He had been terrorizing the Slavic Village area. He had raped something like 20 women in a three-month period.

He had a really weird MO. He would hang out by the corner stores in Slavic Village. He liked petite redheads and blondes. He would always pick them under 5 foot 4, under 110 pounds. He would follow them until they started walking up their driveway. He'd jump out, put a gun to their heads and say, "Don't scream or I'll kill you." He would drag them into his van. He'd lock them in a wooden box in the back of a van. He'd drive to a location, take them out and rape them, put them back in the box, take them right back to their driveway and let them go. He did it to more than 20 women—20 women who reported it.

The guy was in his mid-forties. He had a wife and two daughters and he worked at LTV Steel. He lived in the Lee-Harvard area and had a nice house and a brand-new van. The guy was a monster the way he victimized these women. And none of these women was able to get a plate number.

Finally, he goes to grab a woman and her husband is pulling in the drive. The husband sees the gun, sees the guy trying to grab his wife. He grabbed a plate number and started chasing the guy. Three blocks later, he loses the van but sees me and my partner. He gives us the license number. This is the break we needed. We finally had a plate number. So we broadcast the plate. Three minutes later, a call came over the air that the vehicle was at East 98th Street and Harvard Avenue.

I'm reaching for the mike to say, "Be careful, the guy's armed," when we hear on the radio, "Shots fired. Shots fired." I found out later when they approached his car he jumped out, popped a couple shots at one officer, and took off. This is February, and no fresh snow on the road, but there's patches of ice. It's pretty slick. They chased him down Harvard to Lee, then up Lee to Miles, down Miles to 131st, down to Buckeye.

We're on East 65th and Broadway trying to intersect with the chase. My partner, Jeff Gibson, is driving. To make a long story short, we pinned the guy at East 117th Street and Honeydale Avenue. Jeff said, "Grab the shotgun." He didn't have to tell me twice. It's a standing order in the Fourth District—when you're out on a Code 2 [major fight or weapons out], you jump out with the shotgun, jack in a round, and point it at who you want to listen to you.

So I jumped out with the shotgun and there are six cars on the scene, 10 officers and two supervisors. I'm within 10 feet of the van, yelling at him, "Let me see your hands! Get on the ground! Get on the ground!" He bends down and comes up with a 9 millimeter. I pulled the trigger. Click. It just didn't fire.

He pops two rounds off. The first one goes by my ear, sounding like a circular saw. It barely missed. I dive behind my car and he catches me in the side. Now I'm hit. I know I'm hit but it's not registering. I jumped up from behind the car and put two rounds of shotgun blast into this guy. He goes down. We think the fight's over, right? This is double-ought buck. I'm within 15 feet of the guy. You see bits of the guy coming out of his back when you're shooting. He gets up and starts shooting again. He gets in the van and he's shooting at the police. He plows into two patrol cars, gets out, shoots at another officer who shot him. The guy goes down. Then he gets up and shoots again.

Finally, three to the head put him down and he stayed down. He's dead. Well, he was gurgling and twitching, but he was dead. I'm looking over the dead guy's body. He had 48 entry wounds, according to the coroner's report. Ten officers on the scene, two supervisors, nine officers who fired. One asshole without a vest caught the bullet. I didn't have a vest on. We couldn't afford one at that time. The city wouldn't give them to us.

So I'm standing over this dead guy's body and I've never been more excited and frightened at the same time. I'm shaking, yet there's this adrenaline rush. If I could bottle it, I'd be a millionaire. I'm thinking, "Oh, shit, what the hell just happened?" because it was just that quick it turned. The lieutenant comes up behind me and said, "What's on your back?" I reached down because, honest to God, I thought I shit my pants. As I'm feeling my ass, I feel wet. I'm thinking, "Oh my God, I shit my pants. Do I have a clean pair of pants? Oh my God, I'm a rookie who shit his pants at his first shooting. I'm never gonna live this down."

And I pulled my hand up and it's covered with blood. At the hospital, my partner called my wife. She was six months pregnant. I said, "I gotta tell you I'm okay." And she said "What to you mean,

---

Ten officers on the scene, two supervisors, nine officers who fired. One asshole without a vest caught the bullet.

---

you're okay?" And I said, "I'm okay. I'm at St. Luke's. I'm okay," and she said, "Why are you calling me?" It was past midnight, but she was up because she's always been a night owl. I said, "Honey, I've been shot." She started screaming, "You son of a bitch! How dare you! What a horrible joke to play on me! How could you say this? God forbid you actually got hurt! Hold on, there's somebody at the door, all right?"

Thirty seconds later, she came back and said, "Oh, my God. It's the police. They said you've been shot." I said, "Yeah, honey, but I'm okay." I was lucky. The bullet went in and out of my side. It took a chunk about the size of my thumb out of my side. Three inches more, they said, and I'd be dead.

I went home that night. I decided I was going to quit, that I couldn't do this to her. She said, "If you become a truck driver, you could die in an accident. If you become a construction work-er, you could fall on your head. When you're number's up, it's up. You're still here for a reason. And I don't ever want you to hate me because you had to quit this job. Don't do it for me, because I love being married to a policeman." She's Irish, so there you go.

I kind of went into a depression after I was shot. My wife called Brian Miller, now Seargeant Miller, and he came over one night and said, "Hey, let's go get a cup of coffee." And I said, "No, I don't want coffee." And he said, "No, I'll wait. Get ready. Let's go for coffee."

He wouldn't take no for an answer. We go for a cup of coffee. He sat me down and said, "You know, you didn't die back there. Quit acting like you did." All I needed was to hear that.

JOE SADIE
Captain, Cops for Kids Program

I received a call from another Lawson's store. The clerk, the woman in the store, on Schaaf and Broadview roads said she was getting ready to get robbed. A man is coming in with a stocking mask over his face and a gun. We were told to respond.

So we drive up, turn our lights off, go to the front door. All the lights are on in the Lawson's store and nobody could be seen. I push on the door and it's locked. I can't get in. I take a look to the right and here comes a tractor trailer that says Lawson's on it. I stopped him and said, "Do you have a key to the front door of that store?" He says, "Yeah. I'm getting ready to make a delivery." I said, "Give me the key and stay here."

We call for backup. Backup hasn't gotten here yet. We go in, me and my partner. I said, "I'm going to go behind the counter. You go to the right." He's going up and down the aisles with his gun drawn, looking to see if there's anybody in the store. I'm tiptoeing behind the counter walking to the back room. My partner makes a little bit of noise and it draws this guy out who's in the store. Not only has he robbed the store, he's trying to rape the woman. She's about a 50-year old woman who's obese. She had red hair. And he has her on the floor inside and he's trying to penetrate her, and because she's so heavy he can't get it in. He starts pistol-whipping her, telling her she's too fat to screw. Her head was just blistered with cuts from the gun and she was just covered with blood. You couldn't see where the blood stopped and her red hair began. That's how I remember the red hair.

[Now] he's backing up with his gun to look to see if there's anybody in the store. Ten feet away is me standing there with my gun, pointing at him. And he's got his gun pointing, like, at her, in a different direction. He's shocked to see a policeman. I'm shocked to see a robber. So I yell at him, "Drop your gun." And he turns around and he darts out the door. There's a crash bar. He bolts out the door. Unknown to me, backup arrives and they were sitting out there. And as I start to go after him I hear, *kaboom, kaboom, kaboom, kaboom*! They're shooting at this guy coming out the door with the gun and they're peppering the building.

So I stopped for a second. Then there's no more noise. Now I hit the door and he has run past the police officers that had barricaded themselves with their cars. He runs past them, through them, and he's running down the street. And I come out by the door, and it's the first snow in November. He's dressed in black and there's nothing but white, about threeo'clock in the morning. It was like target practice at the range. Bob Kanzig, standing next to me did the same thing. Bob Kanzig shot him in the arm, I shot him in the shoulder and in the face. He had turned with his gun like this, pointing his gun at me, and I shot him right here. He went down like a deer. We all started a slow jog, and he's laying in the middle of the street. We got within four feet of him and he jumped up and took off. And we lost him in a foot chase on Hillcrest. And so these guys, they're jumping in their car, their driving down the street, and radioing. And me and Bob Kanzig are running and we start to pick up his footprints. I see him. I go to shoot and my gun's empty. So now I've got to stop and I've got to reload my gun. I've got a six-shooter. My fingers are freezing. I'm loading my gun and this guy's running away. So finally we get our guns loaded and now we're looking—we're in a slow walk, back and forth, here and there. And we find blood—he's dripping blood—and we finally find him laying behind a garage, flat, gun in hand. So I said, "Let's get him out and get him to the front and get him to the hospital."

So me and Bob—now it's three o'clock in the morning, guns fired, lights are coming on on Hillcrest Avenue. I think that was the name of the next street over. And people are coming out on their front porch. Here comes me and Bob Kanzig, dragging this guy.

Each guy's got a leg and we're dragging him from the backyard to the front yard. It happens to be garbage day and there's garbage cans on the tree lawns. And we deposit him with the garbage on the tree lawn. Now I have to tell you, if you could see those people, thinking that we just killed somebody and put him out for the garbage man. I looked at those people, huddled up and whispering and talking like this with their hands on their face, their heads back and forth, "Oh my God, what have they done? What are they doing?"

So I said to Bob, "Bob, this don't look good. You better go back and get the car. We've got to get this guy off the tree lawn and get him to the hospital because they're going to say that we put him out here to die." And this guy was bleeding really bad. He said, "That son of a bitch, he—" I said, "I know, but let's make it look good." So he goes and he gets the car. We put him in the car. We had an old sedan. It was an old Plymouth sedan with no markings on it. All it had was the siren. We put the siren on, shot down to the end of the street, made a turn, turned off the sirens and took a slow ride to the hospital. Not only did he live, but I got a call from parole wanting to know if I had any objections to him being put on some kind of a parole. I said, "Absolutely. This guy's got to go to jail."

He went to prison and he lived. The bullet that I shot him in the face with was soft lead. It splattered in his cheek. They left it in there.

CHARLES W. UTLEY, JR.
Patrol Officer, First District

You know, the only opportunity that I've ever had to draw my gun in defense of anybody—my partner or a civilian or myself—was to kill a dog.

My partner and I responded to a call for domestic violence. It was summertime, Madison Avenue at West Boulevard. It was in an apartment. And as we approached this apartment complex, this German shepherd mix comes running out of the very first apartment. So, my partner starts to back up, and I back up and the dog backs up. Neither one of us makes a move, and all of the sudden the dog just goes after him. I don't think the dog even saw me. In a matter of a second-and-a-half, two seconds. My partner was back-pedaling. This dog was on his way to get my partner. I just drew my gun, fired one round, center chest, re-holstered, and the dog went down.

The training at the academy really worked. It was automatic. Just like they trained you. And in retrospect, the only thing I didn't do that I was taught, was to fire two rounds. That's the only thing I didn't do.

There was mayhem after that. The owner comes out screaming, causing a scene, "You didn't have to kill my dog! You didn't have to kill my dog!" The neighborhood just kind of opened up, like, everywhere. They weren't saying anything. The only one who was causing a scene was this guy.

My partner was pretty happy that I got that dog. The dog was pretty close to getting him, two or three feet away from him. I got him at a distance of about 12 feet. Like I said, I don't even think the dog saw me. He was fixed and dialed in on my partner.

WILLIAM TELL
Commander, Sixth District (retired)

Another time I almost got killed was when I was a commander in the Fifth District. It was May 25, 1992. I was working on my boat at the 55th Street Marina. I worked late and I was hungry. I got in my police car—I could take the detective car home—and I started toward McDonald's. As I'm going to McDonald's, I hear the Fifth District police, my policemen, chasing a person in the neighborhood.

I went down Whittier. I go down Whittier and I see this big crowd. Here's a man with a shotgun fixing to shoot another man. I reached for my gun—my service revolver—but I had left it on the boat. I only meant to get something to eat and go back to the boat.

I got out of the car and I grabbed the guy around the neck and I took my other hand and grabbed the shotgun that he had pointing at the man. At this time, the man he was going to shoot tells me, "I know you're Vice." He goes for his pistol and he aims at me. So I kept the shotgun pointed at this guy so he could not shoot me. If he was going to shoot me, he would shoot his buddy in front of me. I wasn't going to let him shoot me.

I finally dragged him to the police car, the whole time, holding this guy off with the shotgun. I was able to call for help, and we arrested him. Guess what? The shotgun I had pointed at the guy didn't have any shells in it. And I got the Medal of Heroism for that. Yep, it didn't have any shells.

MIKE FRICK
Sergeant, Second District (retired)

I made it into the Tactical Unit, when federal funding ran out and they disbanded the Impact Task Force. We would assist Narcotics in all their searches because now we're starting to become a state-of-the-art police department instead of a bunch of ragtags running around. We got a little better training and this was like the stepping stone to the SWAT units they have now.

So one March day we're going on a narcotics raid. It was sunny and the snow on the ground was slushy. We were briefed by Narcotics. The house was a two-story on East 79th off Woodland Avenue and we got the layout. I was an entry guy and the door guy was an officer we called Rebel. He had to go 350 pounds. He was a big old hillbilly with a crewcut and all. He was a ram. We didn't have any of these fancy six-inch pipes with handles on them. He was the guy who hit the door, and if the door didn't go down you knew you weren't going to get through. You definitely weren't going to get through.

So we get up on the porch and Rebel hits the door. Rebel bounced off the door. Everybody's yelling, "Get in! Get in!" I figured maybe two of us should try it, so both of us hit the door and we both bounced off.

When I bounced off, I fell on this tire rim that was on the porch. On the porch is a big window to the living room. I said, "What the hell, we gotta get in," so I picked up the tire rim and I heaved it through the front window and I followed it, figuring everybody else would come in after me.

Well, in front of the window was a portable bar and I hit it and fell face first, knocking it over. There were three guys inside. One had a shotgun, another running up the stairs had a pistol, and the other had a pistol in his belt. As I'm laying on top of the portable bar looking at these guys, I reach for my weapon. It isn't there. At the time, I wore a swivel holster because it was more comfortable when you got in and out of the car. As I went through the window, my gun was unstrapped and it fell out. The next thing I do is point my finger at them and say, "Drop 'em, motherfuckers, or I'll shoot!" Both guys drop their guns with me pointing my finger at them.

They look around and there's Rebel trying to get through this window. He carried a chrome-plated, sawed-off, double-barreled shotgun. As he stepped in, I told him,"Glad you're here, because I'm out of ammo."

BOB TONNE
Detective, Robbery (retired)

I was in the Motorcycle Unit, sometime in the mid-'60s. I was on Cedar Avenue and East 100th Street, and they gave a description of a man who had just robbed a gas station. I saw someone answering the description. I called him over. I said, "Hey, come here." He said, "What do you want from me?"

He sort of caught me off guard. I turned around, I patted him, and I felt a gun by his side. As soon as I felt that gun, he hauled around, turned around and hit me right in the jaw. So I started grappling with him and I'm getting upset with him, and—the rest of the story, some of it isn't clear anymore. All I remember is he said, "Come over here and help me."

The next thing I knew I was on my knees. I looked up at him. He had a .45 in his hand and he hit me right across the middle of the face. I went down. Then he hit me four or five times on my head. There were all kinds of people standing around; I mean, all kinds of people watching him. I woke up. I went to my radio. I was just full of blood. I looked around and there was nobody there.

And I said, "Policeman in trouble on 100th and Cedar." A detective car was one block away. He came over and took me to the hospital. I took stitches—72 of them. I went to Mt. Sinai. He knocked my helmet off when he hit me. But, I went home that night. I don't like hospitals anyway. But I went back to work in two weeks.

BILL SPELLACY
Lieutenant, Fourth District (retired)

Early in my career we were involved in a high-speed chase. I was driving with my right hand and firing my gun with my left. The guy finally crashed, and after we put him in wagon I walked back to the zone car and noticed a diagonal line across the hood. Know what it was? It was where I shot the hood of my own car.

HERMAN SCHMALTZ
Patrol Officer, Second District (retired)

Except for one time, I never had to shoot anyone. And that one time we were shot at. We got him. I caught him right across the knee. The way I can recall it, three guys held up a café on West 65th Street. In fact, the bar was owned by a fellow that I met in the National Guard.

But anyway, we were on West 25th Street, and the call came over. We drove down on Train Avenue, because we figured that was the route the robbers would take. We just got on Train Avenue, and the robbers go flying by us. So we take out after them. The driver goes to Eagle Avenue, down in the Flats, by where old Jim's Steakhouse used to be. I remember them turning the corner and both rear tires are flat. They jumped out and they took off running. We had one right away. He didn't run. The second guy shot at us and missed. And I shot at him and caught him across one knee.

Know what? All the way from West 25th Street, all the way downtown, into the Flats, we were screaming for help, and no help. When that chase ended, our engine was smoking. The top speed, I think, was 40 miles an hour. And after that, the police got a lot of calls about two drunken policemen driving on the sidewalk. It was us. It was the only way we could get around the traffic. We drove

---

After that, the police got a lot of calls about two drunken policemen driving on the sidewalk.

---

on the sidewalk. That was probably in the early '60s, in the summertime. Probably in the morning, close to noon. Yeah, it was on a Friday, because they had the money there to cash checks. Well, when we finally got them all corralled, we searched them all and we found almost all of the money there.

BILLY EVANS
Detective, Auto Theft (retired)

The next time that I was involved in a shooting, I was off duty. It was late '60s and summertime. I used to eat over on East 105th Street and Wade Park. That was a restaurant called Juanita's.

One of the guys from the gas station across the street came and got me. He knew I was a policeman. He said, "See the guy standing at the bus stop?" I said, "Yeah." He said, "He just broke into somebody's car around the corner and took out some tapes and things." I had no idea that this guy had taken a gun out of the glove compartment, too.

So I walked over to talk to him, and as I walked over there, I had a cigarette—I was smoking in those days—I had a cigarette in my mouth, and I saw him standing there with his hand on a gun stuck down in his waist there.

So I said, "Do you happen to have a match on you?" He said,

"No, that's what I need." He had a cigarette also. I said, "Well, okay, then I'll go back over to the gas station and see if somebody there has one."

That was real hard for me to turn my back on someone that had his hand on a gun. I definitely couldn't reach for mine. So I just walked back over to the gas station and got on the phone and called the police to tell them what had happened. When he saw me on the phone, he started running north on East 105th Street. I saw him cut through the medical building lot. I knew there was a high fence behind that building.

So I got in my Pinto, and as I pulled up on him, he was trying to climb this fence with all his stuff in one hand while he tried to propel it with the other one. I jumped out of my vehicle and hollered, "Police." That's when he jumped down and reached for his gun. I shot a couple of shots at him. I aimed for the leg and hit him in the heel. But he was able to run all the way from Wade Park to the first street north of Superior Avenue, which is probably about three-quarters of a mile, before the police caught him. And at the time, he still had the gun in his hand when the police did catch him.

DENNIS SWEENEY
Detective, First District

It was summer of 1986, and there was a gang fight off of Martin Luther King Boulevard and Kinsman Road. One of the kids had a gun. Several of the kids yelled out, "There he is. There he is." I saw the kid. When he saw us, he went down on the ground pretending to tie his shoe. When he did, he set a gun down. I could see the gun. It was a .38, a chrome-plated .38. And I told my partner, "He's got the gun."

I had a line on him with my gun. At that time we had .38s. He was only 20 feet away. I told him, "Don't grab the gun. Don't grab the gun." He picked the gun up. Now at that point, we probably could've shot him, but I could see that he was a 15- or 16-year-old kid. At that point, when he picked the gun up, he turned his back to us and he ran. So, what are you gonna do?

We gave pursuit, but we lost him. There were so many kids. There must've been 200 kids out there fighting. I think we handled it correctly. If the kid would've pointed the gun in our direction, he would've been dead. We would've unloaded. But the fact was that he was young and he never turned toward us when he picked the gun up. He turned and he left.

SEAN GORMAN

Patrol Officer, Ports & Harbor Unit

Tracy Kishler was my partner. Tracy has retired now, but she was 5 feet, 3 inches and 100 pounds soaking wet. We walked into one house where we got a call and the guy we're going to take out is 6 feet, 2 inches tall and weighs 280. I'm thinking I'm going to get my ass kicked and there's no two ways about it. But she talked the guy into the car, closed the door, and said, "Gotcha." You know, it's just a different way of doing things.

KEITH HAVEN

Sergeant, Strike Force, First District

The first time I was shot at was the night with Rob Clark. The night he was killed. I was in the Vice Unit. It was 1998, July 1. Earlier in the night we had received an anonymous call about drug activity at West Boulevard and Madison Avenue, at a particular building. Well, we had some other things set up to do. And it was just a complaint about kids hanging out selling drugs on West Boulevard and Madison. That's very common. Drug activity, street drug sales are all too common.

I grew up on West 80th Street and Denison Avenue. I didn't hang out a lot in the neighborhood, but I knew enough about the neighborhood. I understood. I knew what was going on. You get a lot of complaints—a lot of complaints . . .

We were killing a few minutes before we had to go undercover at a bar. We had a complaint about drug activity at the bar. I was driving. Ray Diaz and Rob Clark were in the passenger seats. Ray was in the back. Rob was in the front. We were in plainclothes but in a detective car. I'll put it this way, the people we get complaints about selling drugs, they identify these cars fairly quickly. We were going east down Madison Avenue by West Boulevard. I said, "Hey, we just got a complaint about this," and I explained it.

And lo and behold, right across the street we see what looked like a drug transaction. And Corey Major takes off. He had a pretty good trot. When he sees our car, it's obvious to us that he noticed something, that we were the police. And it's very common for them to try and hide whatever they have. He's running toward an apartment building. He ran from the south side of the street across the street to the north side to this building. And we kind of focused on him at that moment. And I pulled the car in a driveway, which was, maybe, a building down. It was the closest way to let them out where we could really get on him.

So he went into the building and they chased after him—Ray and Rob. I had to park the car, get the keys, and run down there. And by the time I got down there, I approached the door and it had a metal cover on it. I thought I was locked out. At that moment, it's funny how you can remember certain details at certain times when certain things happen. I thought, "Oh, they locked me out."

And I grabbed the handle and pulled hard trying to get the door open and it came right open. There was a spring on it. So it came open and there's a guy at the top of the stairs shooting at Ray and Rob who are tumbling down the stairs. He's like shooting at them in the back because of the way they're falling down the stairs. Ray fell all the way down the stairs and Rob fell down to the landing. I had to guess that there were about 20 stairs. I could tell Rob was shot. I grabbed Ray's shirt and pulled him and went back to get Rob, and Corey Major was standing at the top of the stairs and started shooting at me. I just returned fire. We exchanged fire and he went down. I ran up and handcuffed him and Ray and I grabbed Rob and pulled him out of the building.

It's hard to keep track when you're involved in something like that. I think I had fired six shots. And that Corey Major had fired six or seven shots, I believe. I'm not exactly sure how many times he had fired over all. But some weird things happen when you're involved in something like that. The way your senses are seeing what's going on. Some things are very distorted. I'm sure you've heard that by now. But, I could hear his gun, see the muzzle flash, but I couldn't hear my gun going off. It's very odd.

Actually, it was almost surreal in the fact that I'm shooting at him and he's just standing there, with no effect. Now, granted, this is probably only a couple seconds, but it slowed down in time. My perception was very slowed down.

Right after he went down, I went up and handcuffed him. I knew that he was shot, but I didn't know how bad he was. I took the gun and put in on the stair where he couldn't get at it. I had his hands handcuffed behind his back. A zone car arrived to assist us. When we got Rob out, I sent one of the officers back in, Herbert Frost. I sent him back in to guard Major, because I didn't know if he was going to get up and take off, or what he was going to do at that point. I found out later that he was dead. I didn't find out until over an hour later.

We kind of commandeered the zone car that arrived. We threw Rob in the car and just drove to Metro Hospital. He wasn't talking, no. He wasn't conscious. I think he was dead right there on the seat. The surgeon—I went back and spoke with him later. He said that had Rob been shot the same way in the Emergency Room, they still wouldn't have been able to save him, and Metro's a great hospital for trauma.

Losing Rob was indescribable. You know, when certain people are in a room, or when certain people are with a group of people, whatever it may be, they change the mood of the room. They change the way everybody is in the room. That was Rob. You know what I mean? It's hard to describe, but when certain people are there, you could have five people in a room and the sixth person walks in, and all of the sudden things are different.

KYLE STOUGES
Patrol Officer, Third District

In the summer of 1998, I was riding with my last field training officer. First District. I was past probation. My FTO was patrolman Al Scott. A wonderful guy, a very good field training officer. You learned a lot just watching him. And we had a rookie, Mike Budny, doing his ride along with us. He was a veteran of the Gulf War. It was the first time he'd ever been in uniform. He was all excited and ready to get going on the job. We pulled out onto Lorain Road and we were at about West 120th when the radio screams, "Officer shot! Officer down! Get EMS here, now! Now! Now!" It was Robert Clark. He was shot and killed.

We were there within seconds. We were one of the first cars on the scene. They were loading Robert Clark's body into the back of a zone car and racing to Metro. It was a pool of blood. The suspect was dead on the stairs. We're rolling up on this and here we've got a rookie in the back. This is the first run of his career. The first run of his career in uniform and an officer getting shot and killed.

It was a long night after that because the whole city was coming down on the area and we had to keep people back to preserve the crime scene. We had to listen to everybody shouting. It was rough. Rough to sit there and listen to it.

TOM ARUNSKI
Patrol Officer, Third District (retired)

In the mid-'70s, two guys robbed a store on Prospect, then they beat up the traffic man at East 4th Street and Prospect Avenue and then they stole a car. So everybody's involved in the chase. It was a perfect summer day. We were all in shirtsleeves. We go past Prospect, cut over to East 30th Street, heading toward East 55th Street.

By this time, guys from the Fourth and Fifth Districts are chasing, too. These guys were shooting out the back of their car at the cops. The lead cop car radioed, "We're receiving fire. They just hit the windshield." Then we're going up Buckeye Road and the Fourth District guys had blocked off the road. The guy hits the brakes, spins around. One guy gives up. The other guy decides to come out shooting. He took about two shots and there were maybe 15 policemen who opened up on him. I'll never forget this as long as I live. There was a haze of blue gun smoke. It was like a fog.

There was a haze of blue gun smoke. It was like a fog. I never saw anything like it in my life.

I never saw anything like it in my life. It was rising above this dead guy with all these policemen around there.

And this black guy comes up. He looks and says, "You guys just killed a soul brother." And a black police officer looked at him and said, "He ain't got no soul now, does he, asshole?"

THOMAS RAFFERTY, JR.
Cadet

The death of one cop still bothers me. Well, one in particular, Johhny Apanittis. His dad was a lieutenant in Cleveland. He was a detective in the Narcotics Unit. This one day in April 1969, he and I were just shooting the breeze. He said, "Well, I'll see you tomorrow, Raf." He had mentioned something about working this part-time job.

Later that day, at home, mom heard the news and asked me if I knew Johnny Apanittis. I said, "Yeah, I just talked to him." She said, "Well, I think he's been shot." I said, "No, I just talked to him. No, he's not."

This was a guy, everybody said, this was a guy you wanted your daughter to marry. He was just a clean-cut, good copper. He went by the book. That's the way Johnny was. Honest. He had a good family; two small children at that time. He was, like, 27 years old at the time.

He was working part-time at Petries downtown. Johnny worked

with another cop, John McNamara. The one clerk had told Johnny, "This male and a female are acting weird. They're in and out. They're looking at things. They're picking things up and putting things back. I think they're getting ready to shoplift."

Well, McNamara came onto the floor. I guess they were working separate floors. McNamara saw the guy put a jacket, or some article of clothing, and conceal it. Well, they grabbed them, a male and a female. The guy stole McNamara's gun. When Johnny came down, McNamara yelled, "He's got my gun!"

John was shot and killed. I believe McNamara was also wounded. They did wound the two suspects. The female went down right there. The guy who stole the gun crawled out and got on a bus. He was caught.

All I did was cry that night.

6.

"Next time, call the Fire Department!"

[STRANGE BUT TRUE]

BOB TONNE
Detective, Robbery (retired)

I remember one time, talk about women, she was only a speeder. I'm chasing her over the Carnegie Bridge. She was going about 60, 65. I'm right behind her with the motorcycle, and I blow the siren. I get along side of her and she starts edging over, trying to get into me.

I get out of the way and she wouldn't pull over, wouldn't pull over. She gets to the end of the bridge and she turns right on West 24th Street behind the West Side Market. And she won't pull over. I yelled out, "Stop." She stopped and I took my motorcycle and dumped it right in front of her. She couldn't move her car.

I go back to the car and I reached in to get the keys. She's screaming and screaming. Her daughter's in the car and she's screaming like crazy. I'm trying to get the keys out, and she's biting and kicking. The woman was yelling, "I'll kick you in the balls! I'll kick you in the balls!" I finally got her handcuffed.

This is summertime. I called the wagon and put her in. I go to court the next morning and she's in court and she's got sunglasses on, a real big fur coat. So I go before the judge, and she pleads not guilty. So I thought, "I'm going to call her husband."

He was a doctor or something. So I called him. I said, "I want to explain to you what happened yesterday. Your wife almost killed me." He said, "Oh, that's nothing. She's been trying to kill me for two years." That's exactly what he said.

DANIEL RUTT
Patrol Officer, First District

My partner and I—it was on Easter Sunday. We were heading southbound on Rocky River Drive by about Larchwood Avenue. There was a truck heading northbound that was probably, I'd say, maybe a quarter-mile down. All the sudden, this motorcycle comes flying up behind it, zips around, and as soon as he sees us he jams the brakes on. Well, he goes head over heels, end over end of the bike on the ground. He landed right in front of our car.

The bike continued skidding down past our car. In fact, there was one guy that just happened to be walking a dog down on the sidewalk at the time, he went home and got his measuring tape. The guy skidded—he started at the VIP Lounge and his bike ended up in front of the dry cleaner there—so it was about 500 or 600 feet that the bike skidded. Remarkably enough, when the guy landed right in front of our car, by the time we got out of the car, he was reaching for his cell phone. His cell phone landed right next to him. He was in pretty bad shape. He had a broken ankle, several cracked ribs, a broken wrist, and his collarbone was broken.

There was a lady that pulled up in a minivan next to him and she yelled out the window, "You got what you deserved." They took him up to Fairview Hospital and, ironically enough, my wife treated him. She's a physical therapist there.

LEE ASHCROFT
Patrol Officer, Scientific Investigations Unit (retired)

Sometimes it gets gory. When you're at a suicide, and a fellow takes a 12-gauge shotgun and he goes to a fence in the back lot on the corner, and he sits down and puts the shotgun up to his throat and pulls the trigger, and there's nothing left of the head, except what looks like a hollowed out cantaloupe. Yes, I would say that's gory.

We've seen them where they've committed suicide and the whole ceiling has been covered with blood. Or they committed suicide and they did it in the bathtub so they wouldn't make a mess, and you're standing on top of that bathtub using a 4 x 5 camera with flashbulbs, and you're photographing down on him, and then as you're getting off the bathtub and you slip on the blood and you fall and your camera falls into the tub. Yeah, I would say that's a little gory.

But, again, it's one of those things that has to be investigated. We used to do all the fingerprinting at the morgue. If a person dies as a result of a homicide and they have a record with us, we would have to go fingerprint the cadaver to close out their file. And it's not routine, but you get used to doing this to a degree. You know the best way to do this and get it done and get out of there.

What's bad is if the body was found floating in the lake and it's almost all decomposed, and you have to try and get prints off in the freezer, and the smell is overpowering. If we got this on a crime scene, we always carry cigars with us. I seem to remember Sunshine Crooks were the favorite brand. And we'd just puff on those cigars all the time until you got done. We never inhaled, but we'd puff like hell to kill the smell.

DENNIS SWEENEY
Detective, First District

We pulled a guy over one night. Summertime, later '80s. There was no traffic and he was moving pretty fast. We had to chase him a bit. And then he pulled over. It looked suspicious as hell, so we approached the car very carefully. The guy in it had a couple pops in him.

On the armrest was one of his testicles. We got him to the hospital as fast as we could. He's lucky he didn't bleed out, crash and die. It turned out he had a whore giving him a blow job and when he didn't come fast enough, she sliced one of his testicles off. The nurse took the testicle in one hand with the glove on, and she's got one of those glass trays. And she turns her hand upside down and the testicle just peeled off in slow motion and hit the plate with a thud. And I looked at my partner and he looked at me and it was the sickest feeling.

You know, he wouldn't tell us who it was. He just wanted to handle it on his own. I told the guy, "The good thing is, you only need one. And you can take the other one home and put it in a pickle jar." But they stitched him up and just threw his nut away.

MICHAEL DUGAN
Captain (retired), Cleveland; Chief of Police, Independence

We had a psych patient who we had picked up at a regular hospital and found that he was an outpatient at Brecksville Psych Unit. Brecksville said that they would accept him and we brought him from Cleveland to Brecksville. And as was customary, you would wait with your patient until the doctor was available to see him, then turn him over to the doctor.

While we were waiting, we have our patient, we're waiting, and an impeccably dressed gentleman in a three-piece, gray tweed suit, nicely coiffed hair, dark on top, gray at the temples, extremely distinguished looking, he starts a conversation with us and we're showing him all the deference of the psychiatrist that we thought he was. Then asked us about prosecuting his landlady who was spying on him when he was trying to come up with a revolutionary textile design. And we realized that the individual who we were calling "doctor" was another inmate!

MIKE FRICK
Sergeant, Second District (retired)

In 1973, I was working day shift with the Impact Unit. We were in the Fifth District. There wasn't as much going on during days as there was on nights. We were cruising East 55th Street and Quincy Avenue and a call comes across about a shooting at East 67th and Quincy.

There was a gas station there at the time. We get up there and, laying in the office area, next to the garage bay, was a guy that was shot several times and bleeding. After the investigation, we found that there was a cheat spot two doors down and he went in to rob it. The problem was that his mother's boyfriend owned the place. In the process of robbing it, the gun battle started. The owner got up and shot him four or five times. At that point, he didn't just drop over dead. He decided to run away. He ran up the stairs, down Quincy, into the gas station seeking help and fell through the glass front door.

Well, work in the gas station never stopped. The owner, the people who were working there, they stepped over the body to get tools, go to work on cars, step over the body to pump gas. I mean, it was like an everyday occurrence there.

The real kicker, though, was while we're standing there, the mother of this boy, the guy who's shot and laying on the floor dead, comes up crying. She's in hysterics. Somebody's trying to comfort her and the next thing we know, after all the photos are taken and it's secured, the mother walks over, grabs the kid, rolls him over, sticks her hand in his pocket and takes out the money. Takes it, sticks it in her bra, and starts to walk away. So now you have a grieving mother and all she cared about was the money that was in his pocket that he took from the cheat spot he just robbed.

JOE ROGERS
Captain, Fifth District (retired)

The riots confused everybody. We tried, but we really didn't have any experience or training. At the Sowinski riots, where the Polacks were throwing bricks and rocks at blacks passing by in cars, I had the paddy wagon. We must have arrested 60 people, and to make it simple we just put my badge number, 326, on the paperwork. So some people pleaded innocent. The charge was disorderly conduct. And as the arresting officer, I have to go to court. So this one big hillbilly, a guy I never even saw before, is pleading not guilty and I'm the arresting officer. After the guy said, "not guilty," the judge said to me, "Officer, what did this man do?" And I said, "He threw a rock," and the hillbilly said, "Yeah, I did. So what?" I could have kissed him.

PETE MIRAGLIOTTA
Patrol Officer, Fourth District

We get a call, 6611 Woodland Avenue, in one of the high-rises there, right there in King Kennedy Projects. There was this big black woman. She's got this butcher knife and she is ranting and raving. She's on the third level and I can hear her screaming. "I'll kill you. I'll kill you, you motherfucker, you bitch, whore, motherfucker." She's just ranting and raving. It's, like, one o'clock. I can't even tell you how hot it was then. It was the middle of the night, but it's one of those nights where it's 78 degrees at one o'clock in the morning.

Well, the bottom line is, she had come back from drinking. Her granddaughter and her granddaughter's boyfriend were fucking. And the old lady stood there watching for a while. The kids didn't know she was there. I said, "First of all, let's put the knife down." I said, "Come on, just put it down." But she said, "No. I'm gonna kill the motherfucker. I'm going to kill him." There's this kid stark naked and there's this girl stark naked. And every time they try to move, she starts screaming.

I said, "Please put the knife down. Put the knife down." But her big beef is that they're not married. She says, "And they're not married. How can he do this?" You really don't have anything. They're all in consent. She walked in and caught her granddaughter fucking some dude. There was no crime. It was consensual, nobody's bitching.

So I said, "If they were married, it'd be okay?" She goes, "Yeah." I said, "Well, I can handle this. Please put the knife down and I'll take of this. I'm going to make you a happy grandma and I'm going to make them a happy couple."

So I get her to put the knife down on the stand. I walk up to them. They're still naked. I said, "Okay, I want you guys to hold hands. Grandma, come over here. I want you to hold my hand over here. I want you two to hold hands and then I want both of you to put your hands on my badge." So they put their hands on my badge. I said, "Okay. By the power vested in me by the City of Cleveland, under the jurisdiction of the Cleveland Police De-

---

She said, "The Cleveland Police Department can marry people?" I said, "Yes, ma'am, they can."

---

partment, you are now . . . ," and I'm going on, "As going forth today, the nineteenth-hundred year of our Lord," I said, "I now pronounce you man and wife."

I said, "Now, because we don't have a marriage certificate . . . here's what we've got to do. What has to happen is, that's only good for a month. So in the month, they've got to go downtown and get their real marriage certificate, but you tell them that they were already married by the Cleveland Police Department, and everything will be okay. And if not, then they can get the annulment and you don't have to go through all that legal work." She says, "Yeah?" I said, "Yeah." She said, "The Cleveland Police Department can marry people?" I said, "Yes, ma'am, they can." She said, "Okay." She sat down. They're looking at us. I said, "Okay, put your clothes on now."

Another time, I essentially did the same thing. These two were beating the piss out of each other. It was in the Fifth District, too. I walked in and they're beating each other up. They're fighting over a dining room set that you would find on a lawn and this little black and white TV. He thinks it's all his. She thinks it's all hers. So I did the same thing. I performed a divorce. Then I flipped a coin after I performed the divorce, and whoever won got the television; the other one ended up with the other thing.

Basically, as luck would have it, he wanted the television. He ended up with the little kitchen set. This is what we're talking about—a set that you find outside. So I give them their divorce. Then I said, "Well, I don't have time. You guys don't have any receipts or anything. I'll flip a coin. Do you agree?"

So he loses. He gets the kitchen set. He starts yelling. I said, "You agreed. You're legally divorced. You're legally separated. You get that." So I said, "How much money do you have on you?" He said, "I got four dollars." I said, "You got four dollars." So I bring it over to her and I go, "Do you really want that broken down black and white television set?" She said, "No." I said, "I'll tell you what. You want this asshole out of your house, right?" She said, "Yeah." I said, "I'll tell you what. He's got four dollars in his pocket. I'm going to make my decision to cover alimony for four dollars. He gets the TV. You get the kitchen set and the four bucks." She said, "Yeah. Man, you police are too smart. I didn't know you'd all be able to do that."

So I said, "Well, I've put in an additional decree. What's going to happen here is, I've reversed my decision on an appeal. You need to give this young lady all the money in your pocket." He said, "That's my four dollars. That's all I got." I said, "She'll give you the television. She'll take the kitchen set and you've got to leave. But you've got to never come back again. If I come back again, you're going to jail." I see him schlepping down the street with this TV, with the cord dangling, bouncing off the sidewalk and he's going down the street.

ANONYMOUS

Twenty years ago, we hear one of the police cars on day shift. It was about 3:30 in the afternoon. They get a call to check for a body under the Detroit-Superior Bridge. I had a lady partner, and we go to assist them.

Now, we get to the area first. We get to West 25th Street and Detroit Avenue. And the wino police are directing us all the way to this body. There's one intoxicated guy standing in the middle of the street. And he's waving us, waving us, waving us north, and he points to the next wino. The next wino's waving to us in front of St. Malachi's and he's pointing eastbound down the hill, right? And so they directed us all the way down. My partner and I, we're standing at the top of this little hill, and we're looking down at this bridge abutment and there's this guy, black male, I'm guessing about 26 years of age, and he's laid out along the bridge abutment, pretty much like you're laid out at the funeral parlor. I mean, it was almost like a cartoon. And it was picture perfect. His fist was up like he was holding a lily on his chest. And it wasn't a lily and it wasn't his chest. He had his hand wrapped around his manhood and he was deader than a doornail.

It's broad daylight, like 3:30 in the afternoon. I'm poking her in the arm. "Partner, I'm the product of a Catholic education, and I demand to know what he's doing down there." She envisioned the undertaker saying, "We'll get his hand off of that thing. We'll chisel it off."

Now, the other car that was supposed to handle this shows up. The one policeman's poking the other one. And he finally looks. The guy had been shot in the head. It wasn't anything real grisly. It was just a little, tiny hole here, and there was what appeared to be dried blood on the front of his shirt. And the one policeman started laughing. He goes, "What do you think that spot is on his shirt?" I said, "Well, all your life your mother's told you that if you touched it, you'd grow hair on your palms. Well, if you squeeze it, you explode."

So, I finally looked at my partner and I said, "We are two women who are not doing some dead guy with his hand on his tool. We are so out of here. We are going to leave it to [the other car] and we're gone." So we leave and we're driving back to the station. I looked at her and I'm laughing so hard, it's hard not to wet my pants. And I tell her, "Partner, it's kind of like a last request. Cowboys want to go out with their boots on. This was a drug deal gone wrong. And he says, I'm gonna kill you now, brother. How do you want to go out? And he says, I want to go out stroking that thing because it's dear to me in life."

So we get back to the station and I call my little old, silver-haired mother who does not want to hear any of these thrilling stories. And I tell her my thrilling police story. And she's laughing. And she finally says, "Honey, you know what? This could've been a crime of passion." I said, "How so, Mom?" She says, "Well, it all depends on whether he came before he went."

FRANK BOVA, SR.
Patrol Officer, Second District (retired)

For the fourth time in a month, we got a call for domestic violence near Lorain Avenue and West 41st Street. The mother had to open the door for us and then went to the kitchen table, crying and sobbing. The wife was all bloody, sitting on the other chair. The father standing against the refrigerator, all bloody, shirt torn up.

I said, "Where's the guy?" She said, "My husband is upstairs, he's going crazy." He came downstairs. He was a tough kid. We fought with this guy. We finally subdued him, handcuffed him, took him to jail.

We had these people come down. They said we used too much violence on the guy. They told the judge that we overstepped our bounds. The father was all whacked out. The mother was all torn up. The wife was bloody. And they said we used too much violence? So I told the father of the guy, "Next time, call the Fire Department."

FRANK BOVA, JR.
Sergeant, Third District

For three months in 1992, I did an undercover operation for Chief Kovacic. We opened a warehouse on East 31st Street and Lakeside Avenue. To make a long story short, we set up this elaborate scheme and word got out that there was a chop shop opening, father and son, from Murray Hill.

Chief Kovacic gave us a Porsche and $6,000 and said, "See what you guys can do over a couple months." The next thing I know, cars start rolling in. We got so elaborate we were taking off the Ohio plates and replacing them with Iowa plates, as if we were shipping them out of state. We told everybody they couldn't come unless they called. But that was because we had other undercover policemen in the warehouse.

One night we get a call and they said, "We've got a really nice Oldsmobile." So they brought it in and sat down and we had beers for them. They proceeded to tell us what they did in this Oldsmobile. The whole thing was on tape. They said, "We stole the Olds and as we're coming out of the lot, we hang a U-turn down by West 3rd Street and a motorcycle cop tries to pull us over. So we go on a high-speed chase. We ran him off the road."

They were laughing and high-fiving. Then they said, "We drove some black family off the road." We found out later the reports had been made. Unbeknownst to us, the car they stole belonged to one of the city prosecutors.

We had a naked calendar there, and in a card file box above that was the camera. We figured if we put a naked girl's picture there, they'd all look at it, so we could get good visuals of these guys. Sure enough, they all stared at it. So we had them perfectly.

They admitted their whole crime spree that day to us. In addition to everything else, we had them for felonious assault on a police officer and felonious assault for running the family off the road.

JIM GNEW
Patrol Officer, SWAT

We had a huge problem with prostitution on Prospect Avenue. We got so tired of taking them to jail and then they'd be out. So Roger said, "Take a ride out." We have five cars loaded with prostitutes and we took them all the way out to Willoughby. We dropped them off in front of a car wash. They're all standing there and we're going back downtown. I thought, "Man, we're never going to get away with this."

The next day, I guess, Willougby had lots of complaints. One of their cars went down there and saw all these prostitutes and said, "What are you doing here?" And they said, "The motherfuckers from Cleveland just dumped us off here. They figured if we walked back downtown we wouldn't have time to do any tricks." It was a fun time. We mixed our work with our fun.

ALAN CIELEC

Patrol Officer, First District (retired)

I used to carry a briefcase with me because I had all my reports, ticket books, flashlight. My dad got it for me when I graduated from the academy. He had my badge number engraved on it.

In 1979, I had two years on the job. Car 111. A station wagon because we hauled dead bodies. A guy's going eastbound on I-90. He wants to get off at West Boulevard. When you come down that ramp, you have to go right or left. He's going too fast and he's too drunk and he can't make the turn, so he goes straight and hits the front porch of a house and flips over. We get there and I had my briefcase in the back seat. My partner said, "You better put your briefcase in the back, by the stretcher, just in case we have to arrest somebody." Well, I thought I knew it all and I didn't.

The car's upside down. We're thinking the guy's gone. As we get closer, we see the rear wheels are spinning, like 100 miles an

---

**He said, "I'm trying to get away."
He's upside down. He's doesn't even
know he's upside down.**

---

hour. We're thinking maybe the throttle is stuck. We walk up to the driver's side and the guy's still in the car and he's drunk. I said, "What's the story?" He said, "I'm trying to get away." He's upside down. He's doesn't even know he's upside down. He's giving it gas and it isn't going anywhere.

I threw him in the backseat. I don't put handcuffs on the guy. I should have. I've got his driver's license and I'm getting information and I hear a hissing noise. I'm wondering if we have a radiator leak or something. He was pissing all over my briefcase. So I ripped him out of the car and put the handcuffs on.

Back at the district, I ripped his shirt off to wipe his piss off my briefcase. I had to take a hose and hose it off. My partner wouldn't help. He said, "I'm not going to help because you should have cuffed him." I had to go down to the basement and hose out the whole back seat of the car. Wash it and dry it.

JEFF STANCZYK
Patrol Officer, Third District

Remember the Wheel Café on Lorain? I can't remember the name of the guy, it was like on 44th. For a million dollars I can't remember the name of the guy that owned it. He shot a bunch of people in there, people trying to rob it and stuff. So we got a call there for somebody shot. So we go in and we look. There's a guy laying on the floor, shot right in the middle of the forehead, and people were stepping over him to play the jukebox. It's like something out of a movie. It's crazy.

* * *

We got a call for a male shot. So we go. An old man comes to the door, "Yes, officer?" We asked him, "Is there some trouble here?" He was an older guy. A kind of mad-professor kind of looking, with the hair. He said, "There's no trouble here. Come in." He goes, "Would you like some tea?" We said, "Well, sure."

We used to take the time with the people. We sat there talking; it must've been 10 minutes. I kept going like this, "Are you sure there's no trouble here? Are you having trouble with anything?" And he would say, "No, officer."

We were getting ready to leave. We were out the door and I said, "We got a call for a male shot." The old guy said, "Oh, well, there's somebody shot here." We said, "Where are they at?" He said, "Well, in here."

We went in this bedroom and there was a young man, 19 years old, laying between the bed and the wall with a bullet in his head. We said, "What happened here?" The old guy said, "That boy's my neighbor and he came over to help me. I paid him to help me pick up my apartment, and he stabbed me. And I shot him."

I said, "He stabbed you?" He took off his robe. He had a heating pad and a gauze pad on his side. I said, "When we asked you if there was any trouble here, why didn't you tell us?" He goes, "There's no trouble here anymore." We took him to the hospital, called the neighbor. This kid had a record a mile long. And he shot him, and the kid fell between the bed and the wall. And that's where he lay.

WILLIAM TELL
Commander, Sixth District (retired)

In the mid-'80s, we got a guy, a Muslim kid, on top of a school— John Hay High School—and he was threatening to jump off. He was despondent. In the old days, if a person was on a house, you didn't wait around. You tried to get him off. If he jumped off, he jumped off. The kid's on top of the school building so we respond there. And we had a fire truck to come with a cherry picker to get this guy off of the school. And every time we'd get ready to get to him with the truck and go near him, he would attempt to jump off, we would stop and pull the truck back.

So we went in the neighborhood and we found some more Muslims. We brought them there and they read the Koran to this guy. They'd read the Koran back and forth. We stayed there so long that the TV cameras left. The only person left there was the reporter from the *Plain Dealer*. So we went in the neighborhood and got his friends. So we're there now from, like, nine o'clock in the morning until three o'clock in the afternoon, trying to be politically correct with this guy on the roof.

So the captain drives up. He said, "Lieutenant, what do you

have here?" I said, "Captain, we've got a guy on the roof. He wants to jump. We don't want him to jump. But every time we bring the fire truck by him, he acts like he wants to jump." The captain said, "Well, move the fire truck over toward him." We moved the fire truck toward this guy and the guy jumped off the roof, down on top of these Muslims. He broke one guy's arm and everything, and he got messed up. I looked at the captain, and the captain said, "Son, you win some and you lose some." He got in his car and he drove off. I said, "You know, I could've done that early this morning if I wanted to."

* * *

Let me tell you about another one. I was a member of the Black Shield Police Association, and we used to meet on East 135th Street and Kinsman Avenue. I lived in that neighborhood. The meetings started at 7:30 P.M. I'm on my way to the Black Shield meeting one night and I see some people walking down the street casing some houses on the next street behind my home.

I went to the meeting and I saw three policemen. So I went to these guys and I said, "Come out real quick. I think these guys on the next street are breaking into some houses." And we go around the street and we were looking. So I get out of my car and I go walking. I don't see anybody. I said, "They're in this neighborhood somewhere."

So they go back between the houses, and all of the sudden, running from the house is a 6-foot-11 black male—a very tall guy. He was running from the three officers and he's running toward me. I'm in plainclothes. So I put my gun up and I said, "Freeze." He stops. He puts his hand in his pocket. I told him, "Take your hand out of your pocket." One of the officers ran up, grabbed the guy's hand, took it out of his pocket. He had a revolver. He was trying to take the gun out of his pocket to shoot me with it, but the hammer was hanging up on the inside of his pocket. That officer saved my life that night.

We were talking to the guy and looked around, and I see another officer coming across the tree lawn, and he's wrestling with this kid. When he came up, it was a midget. This big guy was taking this midget, putting him up to the first floor window of people's houses. He was using this midget to break into houses.

MICHAEL HANEY
Lieutenant, Sex Crimes Unit (deceased)

I was in the Fraud Unit in 1963. We had some pretty sharp people who were shoplifting downtown. Their customers would go into Halle's, look at suits, get tag numbers and sizes and order it from the booster. They'd get exactly what they ordered.

One time, boosters rolled a rack of 20 men's suits right out the door. No one was watching.

There was a woman booster. Her nickname was Track. This bitch could boost anything. She once walked into the detective bureau in the Third District with a car battery. Between her legs. The detectives didn't believe it.

ROBERT LEGG
Lieutenant, Third District (retired)

It was 1972, off East 92nd, male stabbed. Midnight, summer. We took him to the hospital and learned his wife had stabbed him during an argument. We asked him if he wanted to prosecute her—this was before the domestic violence laws that demanded prosecution. He said no, he loved her. That was either the 27th or 28th different time she had cut him during an argument. I really don't know if he loved her that much, or if he just couldn't take a hint!

HERMAN SCHMALTZ
Patrol Officer, Second District (retired)

A woman calls up and her husband's beating her up—right on State Road. I'll never forget her. We pull in there. Get out and walk in. Yeah, he's slugging her. I grabbed a hold of him, trying to get the cuffs on him. The next thing I know, she's on my back, punching me in the back and pulling my ears and scratching me. She said, "Let him alone! Let him go!" We wound up throwing them both in jail. And that happened to me one other time, until I learned— wait, don't rush, take your time, until they both get tired.

MICHAEL DUGAN
Captain (retired), Cleveland; Chief of Police, Independence

There was a female lieutenant and a patrol officer involved in a funny case. It was the early '80s. Both are still on the job in Cleveland. She's still a lieutenant and he's still a patrolman. There was a case that an individual was caught, I believe it was in his garage, having sex with a chicken. The officers promptly arrested the individual for cruelty to animals. Because of the unusualness of the incident, they called their fairly newly promoted female lieutenant, who wasn't quite worldly, especially on issues with animals. They had relayed the information. She had said that the proper statute that they should arrest for was cruelty to animals. As an aside, she had asked one of the officers, "Was it a male or female chicken?" The officer indignantly replied, "He's a pervert, not a queer."

JAMES MCMANUS
Patrol Officer, Impound Unit

People who come to the Impound Unit to get their cars don't care if it's been there 30 days or 3 years, when they decide they want to come and get it, they want it to be there.

I had one guy who came in and he wanted to know if we towed his car. We said, "Yeah." He gave us the plate number and said, "What do I have to do to get my car?" So we explained to him that he needed his license, proof of ownership and all of that. He said, "No problem. How much money do I need to get it out?" At that time, he had had it towed in rush hour and it was a over a hundred and some odd dollars. The guy threw his hands up in the air and he did a 360 and he stopped right where he started, basically, and he passed out—right on the floor.

And all the customers in line were just looking at him. The young lady who was working with me at the time was still explaining to him the directions to the lot, and he's laying on the ground—out. She said, "And you need to sign this release form." So she walked around the corner with an ink pen to hand it to him to sign. She said, "Oh, well." So she came back in. The people in line were stepping over him and they start up their tirade about their cars.

Meanwhile, the guy was on the ground. It was just so busy at the time. She said, "Do you think maybe we should get an ambulance for him?" I said, "Yeah, I believe so." So we called and they came. By then, the guy had come to and they were asking him what happened. He said that the shock of finding out how much his car was caused him to have a sickle cell anemia attack. The EMS people said that they had never heard of that. They trotted him out and we proceeded with business as usual. The next customer would come with their tirade and that's how it's always been down there.

TOM ARUNSKI
Patrol Officer, Third District (retired)

I was assigned to a Strike Force when the city got some federal money. They'd make up these units and they'd last a couple years. We would handle only felonies. One day my partner and I were working in the Fifth District and we get a call on a bank robbery on Euclid Avenue at East 101st Street.

We pull up and we're the first car there. The people in the bank were shook up. One teller told me, "You have to understand what I'm telling you. A midget came in the bank and handed us a note that said give him money or he was going to hurt somebody." The robber was handed a bag of money. When I asked how much money was in the bag, she said a couple hundred bucks and, "He walked out the door. It was a black midget and he's wearing tan pants and a checkered coat."

We drove around the corner and here's this black midget with a money bag next to him, hiding behind a fire hydrant. He put his hands in the air and said, "I give up! I give up!" Before the FBI came and snatched him, I asked him why he would rob a bank. He said he lost his job and needed the money.

MICHAEL DUGAN

Captain (retired), Cleveland; Chief of Police, Independence

Somewhere in the early '70s, an officer working the Seventh Precinct at Jones and Broadway—it was a substation of the Fourth District—filed an Injury on Duty report. He was coming up the stairway, and coming down the banister in the opposite direction was a rat. The rat bit him on the stomach, and this is the official version that initially went down in his story. Probably 20 years later, I talked to this officer and found out the true story. He was coming up the stairs, saw the rat eye to eye, pulled out his service revolver, fired point-blank at the rat and missed, the rat jumped and bit him in the stomach.

TOM DIEMERT

Sergeant, Fifth District (retired)

A bank robber came into a Cleveland Trust on East 152nd Street and School Avenue, in Collinwood. We got an alarm and we pulled up. I came in and I was looking around and nobody seemed very excited. Turns out the guy walked up to a teller and told her it was a bank robbery and she said, "So, where's your gun?" The guy panicked and ran out.

* * *

I went to the Vice Squad and after that to the Mounted Unit. I loved horses. I owned a horse when I was a kid. When guys were buying fancy cars or hot rods, I rode a horse.

It was the summer of 1970 and my beat on the horse was the City Hall beat. It went from West 9th Street to East 9th Street, from Lakeside to Superior. It was a big route. The troop might be 20 guys and we'd go down Lakeside Avenue and peel off to our beats. But I peeled off and went to Playhouse Square. I had to get something. I tied the horse behind the theater, walked up to the corner, and I'm standing at the corner and there was a lot of water going down the curb. I saw a piece of paper floating at the curb and I said, "That looks like a city payroll check."

I bent over and picked it up. The name on it was Steve Diemert, my brother. He was in a different firehouse but they called him— he wasn't even supposed to be there—to put out a fire on a theater marquee. While he's doing that, he lost his check. Neither one of us should have been there. What are the chances?

SHAWN KNIERIEM
Patrol Officer, Canine Unit

My [police dog] Shiloh was a real character. He was extremely food-motivated. He didn't care much for finding drugs, but a baloney sandwich? He was right on it! I used to bring him into the office where he would sniff out the crew's lunches and paw at the desk drawers until he got them opened. Usually he was rewarded with a treat. He especially loved apples. You'd throw him one and he'd eat it like a horse.

This particular night, he started sniffing around a counter which had drawers underneath. I knew no one kept any food in them and that's what I told Shiloh. He kept sniffing and pawing and would look at me and bark. Finally, I got exasperated and threw open the drawer. To my shock, a huge rat jumped out and started scampering across the floor.

Shiloh was overcome with joy. Almost pulling my arm out of its socket, he took off after this rat, who, by now, had located the doorway which led out to the lobby where the citizens waited to file reports. Needless to say, when the citizens saw a gigantic rat, being chased by a salivating German shepherd, they all decided they had better things to do with their time and proceeded to stampede out the front door.

To Shiloh's dismay, the rat disappeared behind the vending machine.

The next night I was in the office telling this story to my coworkers when Shiloh dragged me over to the same drawer and started pawing it. I knew he was just keyed up by the smell and I tried to ignore him. He became so obnoxious one of my coworkers went over and threw open the drawer. I was just about to announce to

---

When the citizens saw a gigantic rat being chased by a salivating German shepherd, they all decided they had better things to do.

Shiloh, "See, no rat?" when the same rat jumped out of the same drawer and, having run this route before, straight into the lobby. Once again, the rat, Shiloh and I emptied the lobby. And the rat disappeared behind the vending machine. This time, never to be seen again.

* * *

When you get a call for "unknown trouble," or "some kind of trouble," these can be the worst, so my partner and I didn't know what to expect when we pulled up one summer day. The tenant was outside and she looked scared. We asked what we could do for her and the conversation went like this:

Woman: He came in the through the front door.

Us: Who?

Woman: He's in the house now.

Us: Who?

Woman: He's in the bedroom.

Us: Who? (We're starting to sound like owls at this point.)

Woman: Cat.

Us: Cat? Who is he to you?

Woman: He's a cat.

We finally get the information. A cat had jumped through her door—no screens, of course—and she wanted it out of her house.

We located the cat behind a dresser. I asked for a towel, dropped it over the cat, scooped it up and took it outside and let it go. It was probably back inside her house before we drove away, as she didn't both to shut her inner door. But we didn't hear from her again.

TOM ARUNSKI
Patrol Officer, Third District (retired)

Harry [Liesman] liked to drink downtown. And when he drank downtown, he always wore a suit and tie. Anyway, a bunch of us are at the Town Pump on East 9th Street. We're all drinking on discount. No uniforms; we were all off duty.

And there's one clown at the far end of the bar who wants to get involved in the conversation because we were all bullshitting and telling stories. Most of us were trying to impress the barmaid, who was pretty good looking. The guy at the end of the bar is getting frustrated because we're not letting him in on the conversation and he starts giving Harry a bad-ass look. And I'm thinking, "Uh-oh, pal, you're picking on the wrong guy."

Harry looked back at the guy and said, "Is there a problem?" and the guy said, "Oh, you fuckers are all alike." He started ranting and raving and he said, "I don't believe half the shit you're telling tonight." With that, Harry takes out his gun and I thought, "Holy shit! I'm supposed to be home with my son!" Harry takes a bullet out of the cylinder and slides it down the bar, spinning right in front of the guy. Then Harry said, "The next one's coming at you . . . a little bit faster." The guy took off out the door.

That was the last time I drank with Harry Liesman.

KYLE STOUGES
Patrol Officer, Third District

We responded to a call to assist EMS off West 130th Street, south of Bellaire Road. It was a male with an explosion burn, possible other ordnances involved. We show up and there's a guy in the garage, laying there, screaming, with EMS trying to hook him up to all the stuff. He's bleeding profusely from the midsection.

What happened was, he went on the Internet and asked how to make a bomb. He mixed fertilizer and all this other stuff. Well, he had the jar between his legs to hold it steady while he's mixing. He didn't read far enough ahead, I guess, where it said not to mix the ingredients. Sure enough, an explosion.

They said he was going to have surgery. I think he could join the transvestite ranks. I did ask him, "What were you thinking?" And he said, "I just wanted to make a bomb."

* * *

We arrested one transvestite whose street name was Tameka, but whose real name was Tim. He was about 6 foot, 4 inches, and easily 250 or 260. Breast implants, wig and everything. We had arrested him before and that's the way we did it. We built a case. We arrest them so many times for soliciting and then, when we go to court, we say, "Your Honor, this person has been arrested four times for soliciting and it has to stop."

Anyway, we get to the Second District jail, which is an all-male jail. He's a man, so he has to be put in the male population. There must have been 30 males in the front cell, ready for the transport unit to come. They started whistling and yelling, "Woo-hoo, baby!"

There's a concealed cell for males who are extremely violent or have some kind of contagious disease that prevents them from being with the general population. And in it that night was this crazy homeless guy. When we walk in with Tameka, or Tim, the [homelss] guy drops to his knees and says, "Please put him in here with me. Put her in here with me. Put him in here with me." He's ranting and raving on his knees, like he's praying.

And Tameka says, "Please don't make me go in there with him." Well, then as we're getting Tameka/Tim's property, Tameka says, "I can't take this bra off." I said, "You're a male. You can take the bra off." He said, "Don't make me take off the bra in front of all these men." So I took him around the corner and he took it off and we walked back.

We hadn't heard anything from the homeless guy in the cell when he finally said, "I gotta tell ya, Officer, that clothing screams woman, but those shoes scream bad!" He was referring to Tameka's feet, which were easily 15 or 16.

JOE SADIE
Captain, Cops for Kids Program

In 1977, I was a patrolman in the Second District, which was before portable radios. Car thieves were stealing Chevys like crazy. They'd pop the ignition and start it with a screwdriver. What they'd be doing was, they'd steal it, take it and strip it for parts, then get in their own car and go. They didn't want to stay in the car too long.

We had tons of those. I was a young policeman then, a pretty good runner. I could run down anybody. We ended up in a chase where these guys bailed out of a stolen car. They bailed out of the car and I chase him. I'm going through yards, jumping over fences, yada, yada, yada. It was the lower end of the West Side. I finally come across this kid in a full gallop, crouched down behind something, and I don't know what he's got. And I've got my gun out. I come up on top of him and I'm almost running past him.

I whack him on the head with my gun. He takes off. He went over one fence and his pants got caught. He left a patch of his pants on the fence and I grabbed it and stuck it in my pocket. The kid was fast. He got away.

Now I'm mad, and furthermore, I don't know where I am. I mean, I know the neighborhood, but I couldn't tell you what street I was on. But that's not a problem. My partner went after the driver and he'll be coming for me. So I walk to the street and look up and think I see the kid I was chasing. It's long ways up, but I think it's him. Well, we don't have portable radios and I don't have a car. But there's a car coming up the street, so I step out in the street and stop it. I get in; tell the guy I need help catching the kid at the far end of the block. I told the driver to tell me when we were close and I got down on the floor of the car. The driver told me when we were close and I thanked him and told him to take off. I jumped out and grabbed the kid. It was him. The piece of cloth I took from the fence fit the hole in his pants.

So I arrest him and handcuff him. We wait for my partner to come around, and finally he does. We get the car thief in the back seat. While we were driving in, he started telling us that he had nothing to do with it, that it was the other guy, that he was just along for the ride. I said to him, "That's too bad. Because I caught you. If I don't get the other guy, I don't care. You're gonna own it all." He was scared. I said, "I'll tell you what. I'm a man of my word, if you help me get the other guy, I'll go easy on you. I'll help you out. When we go to court, I'll tell the judge," and so on. He thought about it and thought about it and then finally he said, "Okay." I said, "Who's the other guy?" He said, "The guy that dropped you off!"

7.

"Can I touch your badge?"

[IN THE COMMUNITY]

FRANK BOVA, SR.
Patrol Officer, Second District (retired)

Me and Sam Ballomo were driving along East 55th and White Avenue when a call came for a holdup on Wade Park, which is a hell of a long way from where we were. I said, "Let's just drive that way in case something happens." So they give a description of the robber. It was a holdup in a delicatessen.

By then, we're at Superior Avenue and East 83rd Street. So we see a guy, and the description is not even near what this guy looked like walking down the street. But something told us there was something wrong with this guy. It was wintertime and we had those big coats with the big pockets. We pull in behind him and said, "Put your hands in the air." I had my gun drawn. Just something in our guts that said something was wrong.

So I walk up toward the guy and he leaps at Sam and puts a gun to his head. I put my gun to his head. He said, "You're not goin' to trade your partner's life, so put your fucking gun down." I said, "Well, I'm not too sure that you're going to shoot him, but you don't want to die, do you?"

So I talked to him for I don't know how long, and something told me Sam was going to do something. I worked with Sam for five years. He hit the guy's wrist and slid. I hit the guy over the head with my gun and hit him again and he fell to the ground. And when he hit the ground, all the stolen money started falling out.

And here comes this little old guy coming through the parking lot and he's screaming at us, "What are you doing here?" I said, "Get the fuck out of here!" We were trying to subdue this guy. So we subdue the guy, we arrest him and we go to court. It was in front of a woman judge. She said she didn't know who to believe.

Who do you think popped up in the back of the courtroom? The guy I told to get the hell out of there. He comes up and tells the judge exactly what happened. He had followed the case. So I took him out to lunch, shook his hand and said, "Man, you're a hell of a guy." You just never know.

JOE SADIE
Captain, Cops for Kids Program

Let me tell you why I started Cops and Kids. I was in the Inspections Unit as a lieutenant, and I get a complaint. Our SWAT Unit, which they often do, took somebody's door down and humiliated some young man.

What happened was, we were looking for a guy that shot a police officer. It was a summer day in 1981. We go to the projects on Kinsman Road. We knock on the door and this young man comes to the door. The SWAT team had surrounded the apartment; guys behind trees with guns and so on. And then they had the Entry Team that goes up to the front door. The Entry Team meets this young man, who opens up the door. There's a screen door between them. And they ask for this guy. The young kid's sort of startled, baffled by all of this. And he doesn't answer them. Now they're thinking that the guy with the gun who shot this policeman is on the inside of the house behind this kid. They grabbed this kid. They yanked him through the door and threw him down the stairs where the Cover Team's at. And they get him kneeling on the grass with his legs crossed and his hands behind his head. And then they fall back and have him sitting there. They enter the apartment. They go through it and he's not there. They got the wrong apartment.

They had the wrong address.

This is in the summertime. You had 100-plus people—this is a black neighborhood—watch them go in and humiliate this kid. Now, what do you think they do when they leave this apartment? They get in their cars and they leave. The kid's still kneeling on the grass in the same position they put him in. And they're gone.

So they made a complaint, and I got the complaint. The kid was about 15 or 16 years old. So they make a complaint. I go to the projects. I'm in uniform. They're somewhat impressed. They've got a uniformed officer sitting there talking to him. They say, "Well, somebody's listening." So I listen to the story. Obviously, they're looking for a little bit of their dignity back, some respect.

I got all my complaints in my two years of being in that unit withdrawn. I would get them to sign a withdrawal slip, no longer requesting an investigation. That's how well I did satisfying the complaints. My secret is spending a lot of time talking to them and giving them back their dignity, genuinely letting them know that we were apologizing and trying to give them an explanation.

This is what I did with this kid. I took this kid to the SWAT Unit and showed him what they did. Then I took this kid to the Safety Director, who, at the time, was Reginald Turner, and took him on a tour of City Hall. I got him a summer job. And then for five years after that, I paid for their Thanksgiving and Christmas dinners, until I got transferred out of that district, the Fourth District.

I never saw that kid again, after I got transferred. He grew up. He ended up going to college. He ended up getting a job working for a radio station as a deejay of some type. I ran into him. I didn't recognize him, but I looked the same. He recognized me. He came up to me and he gave me a big hug. He said, "I'm 'so and so.' You used to buy us Thanksgiving and Christmas dinners. Do you remember me? You got me a summer job."

Well, you know what? That was the roots of Cops and Kids.

* * *

The organization helps anybody. When they had a couple of policemen killed in Garfield Heights, a few Christmases ago, they called me up. One policeman had a family with children. They knew we take care of kids. They said, "Can you help us?" And from that day forward, Garfield police come with us at Christmas and we go to the hospitals and day cares and do it on one day. We have a roll call of Santa Clauses, about 13 or 14 Santas. We do about 2,500 kids just in that one day.

I also do it all year long. I do child gun safety. I do "How to use 911." I do field trips with sports players, like the Cleveland Indians. I take the kids to the Gund Area, to the circus, to the ball games. I got a bunch of kids going to the Browns game when they play Pittsburgh—25 kids.

The criteria for the dream seats with the Cleveland Browns was, we have to teach kids about staying away from drugs, smoking, and booze. So I sent police officers into a certain classroom to give the kids four or five weeks of training, and for that, they get rewarded by the Cleveland Browns. Cops and Kids is the vehicle that delivers it. You got uniformed officers helping the kids.

When I got involved, they were trying to raise money for Christmas, and they were doing a golf outing and they couldn't sell tickets. So Chief Kovacic said to me, "Can you help these guys out? You're pretty good at that." So not only did I get involved in helping with that golf outing, but I took over the program and changed it, from one day a year to 365 days a year to Cops and Kids.

It's volunteer. Nobody gets paid. It's a 501(c)3 charity. It's supported by businessmen mostly. Policemen donate at Christmas time. Our department sends out a departmental notice and the policemen donate. But I have a board and the board members write checks between $5,000 and $20,000 apiece.

Well, for 10 years, probably, I had to struggle with this program, probably gotten demoted from commander to captain because of it. Mike White did not want me doing this program. He said it was not a part of my duty. The chief wanted me to do this because it gave a positive image. It got great press. Finally I got demoted with five other guys one day. I was warned several times by the chief, "Keep it down. Keep it down. Don't do any interviews. Try to stay off TV." The mayor was fighting with the Police Department and the union. And I was making the Police Department look good. I was on the command staff. I was supposed to be on the mayor's side.

So it cost me my job as commander, but that was irrelevant. This chief sees the value. And this mayor has called on me numerous times to do stuff for her—with an Easter egg hunt, and with hanging the ornaments on a tree in the rotunda at City Hall, where I would take care of the children with treats and stuffed animals. And bring the Easter bunny—police officers dressed as Easter bunnies, and as other characters at Easter, like I did this past year when she had her Easter egg hunt, horse-drawn carriage.

So the chief put me in charge of charitable organizations—executive officer in charge of charitable organizations, is one of my duties, which to me is a path to do Cops and Kids. Basically, all I do now is Cops and Kids. All my waking day is Cops and Kids.

* * *

I want to talk to you about the value of this program, taking children that are that young and building a bridge for the Cleveland Police Department, especially where we are known in some places as the occupation force. Guys in black uniforms, taking down doors, pulling out loved ones, and never taking the time to explain why we were there, even though he might've been wanted for murder or dealing drugs. All they know is they love him, and we're the guys, the evil bastards, who went in there and broke the door down, and now the house is cold because it's winter time, and their father's gone.

So we need public relations like no other division does, certainly not the fire department, who are seen as heroes, carrying people out of burning buildings. So here we are—put this in perspective—a little boy walks up, a little Spanish boy, whose mother and father probably tell him, "If you screw up, I'm going to turn you over to the police." We're like the bogey man in the community. Did you ever hear that? Did you ever see that in a shopping mall? "I'm going to have to tell that policeman on you."

So here we are. This is the syndrome. The little boy walks up to me and he tugs on my jacket. It's in the wintertime. We're wearing a black leather jacket and we've got on a hat. And the little boy says to me, in broken English he says, "Can I touch your badge?" And so I knelt down. So now I'm face to face with this little guy. I said, "Sure. Touch my badge." I wasn't thinking anything of it until the next question, "Does your hat come off?"

Let me tell you what that told me. I wasn't a part of the community. I was a soldier, something that doesn't sleep and eat, something that doesn't have a family. I'm this thing that's out there in the street, this soldier, part of the occupation force, the bogey man. He didn't see me as a human being. I took my hat off. Somebody comes by and takes my picture. I don't think nothing of it. I see the picture when it gets developed and I say to myself, "That's that

---

We're like the bogey man in the community. Did you ever hear that? Did you ever see that in a shopping mall? "I'm going to have to tell that policeman on you."

---

little kid." And then it hit me. Here he is with the hat on his head, smiling, and I'm holding him.

And I'm thinking to myself, "That's what this program's all about. It's about coming down to their level; letting them know that we're mothers, fathers, aunts, uncles; that we're people that care. We love children. And we're not bad people.

ALAN CIELEC
Patrol Officer, First District (retired)

So me and my partner are going north on West 130th Street. We came to Lorain Avenue and stopped for the light. The guy was going eastbound Lorain. Instead of stopping at 130th and making a right-hand turn to go south, which was his intention, he goes up on the sidewalk between a phone booth and a bus stop. I looked at my partner and said, "Did you see that? I don't believe that."

We were the first car at the light, so he had to see us and he did it right in front of us. I made a U-turn, turned on the lights and siren. But I made the turn so aggressively that my front right tire hit the curb and I got a flat. But the guy we were chasing didn't know it. He pulled over. Had he not pulled over, we never would have caught him because I was in no condition to chase him.

My partner and I were aggravated. We figured this was our quitter. We're going to book him and we're going home. So we searched him and put him in the back of car. We hardly ever put violators in the back of the car. It's unsafe because you search them and if you're in a hurry, you could miss something. So my partner is the passenger and that means it's his job to write the ticket.

As my partner's getting the information, the guy hands me a courtesy card. I tear it in half and toss it in the ashtray. I said, "No courtesy card is going to help you." But something told me to look at the card. Who issued it? Emil Cielec. My dad. I said, "Stop writing."

I asked the guy how he knew my dad. He said, "From my father. He's the upholstery guy, that does upholstery for cars." My dad has a couple antique cars and the guy did a lot of work for him. And I said, "Okay, I know your dad. You ought to thank God it was me and my partner who pulled you over because anyone else would have torn the card up and either written a couple tickets or towed your car. You go home and tell your dad that I stopped you because I'm gonna call your dad to find out." So you know, you bend the rules. There's a time to arrest somebody and a time not to arrest somebody.

GARY EUGENE KANE
Sergeant, Strike Force, Sixth District

I remember when I first got on the job, and I was still fairly new, the first year or two, there were a lot of people from Appalachia in the Second District. I remember going to some kind of family call, some kind of family trouble on West 14th Street and Clark Avenue. This was in the summertime, in the middle of summer, a bright sunshiny day.

And we go down there, me and my partner. It was a lady and, like, 4 or five 5 from the age of, probably, I want to say, from the ages of 14 to 5 years old. I remember there was one little brown-haired girl. My partner's talking to her. I'm just looking at them and I'm thinking, these people are straight out of Li'l Abner. The Li'l Abner comics.

And just when I'm thinking that, I hear the little girl, she leans over to her brother and she's looking at me and she says, "They give them guns," talking about me being a black man. "They give them guns up here." It just shows you how people look at things. That little girl was probably about five or six years old. I always remember that, too. It comes to me when people start stereotyping, racial things. Too many things are certain things you get from your parents. But you've got to overcome. I try to take people for what they are after I learn about them. I don't believe in walking in there with blinders on and just accept anything that someone says. You can't do that. You expect certain things from the way a person carries themselves or how they dress or what they have on.

DENNIS WONDRAK
Patrol Officer, Fourth District

A little after 9/11, I was making a traffic stop on East 131st Street and Marston Avenue and a woman was backing out of her driveway. She said, "I just want to thank you for being out here." That meant the world to me.

My partner, Mark Lipnick, and I were arresting some dope boys on the corner. It was late at night, 11 or midnight, and as we were putting them in the car, people on their porches started clapping. It was as if they knew what they saw. They knew what those dope boys were doing and they [knew] the police did something. That meant a lot.

KYLE STOUGES
Patrol Officer, Third District

We had busted [this one guy] so many times for selling phony crack rocks, fake rocks, to a lot of drug addicts. He'd sell them anything from peanuts to cracker crumbs. And they'd buy them. We told him, "If you keep doing this, someone's going to get angry and you're going to get shot." Sure enough, not three days after we told him that, someone hunted him down and shot him in the chest. He almost died. He's back out now and just as ignorant.

JEFF STANCZYK
Patrol Officer, Third District

We have in Cleveland the Citizen Police Academy, where people can go through a cut-down version of our police academy. There are eight weeks of classes. They go to the range. They go for a ride-along. They get instructions by different coppers. I'm one of the policemen that does that.

And I tell the story of the man who, just a few years ago, butchered his children. Their bodies were in the bathtub and their heads were on the stove. And I talk about the police officer who walked into that insanity. I want to make a point. There are reasons police throw up walls. Working cases like that would be one of them.

People come up, and I'll shake hands with everybody in that room, and I'll say, "Now, what did you touch? You didn't touch metal or stone. You touched another human being." But as a police officer, you're held to a higher standard. You're supposed to be stronger, faster, smarter. We're just people doing a job, man. But you're supposed to, when you see a copper going by with some kind of stone cold face, you don't know where he just came from. You don't know what he just did. And you're supposed to be

Mr. Public Relations when you come on to your next run, because you don't miss a beat. You don't miss a beat.

* * *

I was a DARE [Drug Abuse Resistance Education] officer for six-and-a-half years. I enjoyed it. I love the kids, but it's hard on your heart. These are elementary school kids. DARE lets the kids see policemen in a different light.

You know, you always hear the parents or people saying, "If you're bad, that guy's going to put you in jail." They don't see that you're somebody they can go to for assistance. I worked a real bad school, Longfellow, off of East 156th Street between St. Clair Avenue and Lakeshore Boulevard. I used to take kids out of there in handcuffs. These are elementary school children. They were busting windows out of doors with their fists. Four fourth-grade kids jumped on a teacher, a librarian, and beat her in the face with books and broke the orbital bones.

Parents would come and threaten the principal with a knife. And I wasn't there for enforcement. But if you called me, I'd go. The kids there, a lot of kids, we had an understanding. I would do my thing. They would be respectful during my class and they would do whatever else they had to do. Because I used to do magic and stuff to get the point across.

I got a call once. It was the early '90s. I heard [a] call come over the P.A., "Officer Stanczyk, report to the auditorium." I was one of the first four DARE officers in the city of Cleveland. So we went to the auditorium, and every kid in the thing was in there. The principal said, "We want you up here on the stage." I walked up there. I didn't know what the hell was going on.

She gave me a note and it said, "Officer Stanczyk"—and I've got the note framed at home—it says, "You told us you couldn't afford a bullet-proof vest." (Because this is before they issued us vests. If you didn't pay for it, you didn't have a vest.) It said, "Please take this because we love you." It was a shoebox. And I opened it up, and there was, like, $878 in cash in that box for me to get a vest.

And even the kids I took out of that school were standing up and applauding.

Understand this, it could've been any of us. It just happened to be me. I told them, "I appreciate this. But I can't take this money." I said, "You take this and put it in your drug fund, or whatever you need. But I'll keep this letter."

It's like, the people don't understand what good you can do in this uniform.

SEAN GORMAN
Patrol Officer, Ports & Harbor Unit

I work late. You don't get to see nice people on midnights. You get to see all the dirtbags. We worked the Kinsman beat for a while. We handled one block on either side of Kinsman from the length of it. And you know what? Between midnight and four o'clock in

---

I work late. You don't get to see nice people on midnights. You get to see all the dirtbags.

---

the morning, every time we stopped a car, either nobody had a driver's license, or they had warrants, or they had dope in their car or they had a weapon in their car. That's what you got. That's where you're at. That's what you deal with. You don't get to deal with the nice guys in the neighborhood until six A.M. when they come out and find their cars stolen and they have to get to work.

HOWARD WISE
Police Photographer

In 1966, we organized a Cleveland Police softball team, all Cleveland policemen. Joe Jezior was the manager. We were playing in the Brookside League. And we just ran over it. We were just all very talented ballplayers. Remember, there were 2,000 guys to draw from. We found some good ballplayers. We took it seriously. We didn't go there to lose. We got some nice trophies.

We threw our guns in a bag when we played. We played one night at Woodland Park at about 11:30 at night. We were playing in a citywide tournament at Woodland Park. Our manager walked in with his bags and he could hardly carry it. That's how heavy it was. There were 15 guns in there. And we won.

Then we joined the Cleveland Police Industrial League team. We had Ford, White Motor was in there, the Local 1250, Local 507, the Cleveland Fire Department. That was a nice league. We were in it for 23 years. It was a very nice bunch of guys. A great bunch of ballplayers—I was the pitcher. But I was the manager in 1974 and '75. We went to the World Tournament two years in a row. We won the division here. That was the Industrial league. You all had to work together. We saw some great ball seasons, I'll tell you.

TOM DIEMERT
Sergeant, Fifth District (retired)

In the '70s, WERE-AM was an all-talk station and they had a show by Count John Manalesco. He was doing some things about police work that just didn't seem right to me, so I called him up.

And I was talking to him and he said, "Hold on, I want to talk to you off the air." He asked me to come on his program and I thought, well, I can't back down now. So I did. It was very good. He was good and he was enlightened by a lot of the things that we were able to tell him that were really happening. And there was a lot of controversy then, the Vietnam War, the riots, strikes and what policemen did and what the work was. The following Monday, I got a call from Penny Bailey, who had a show, too. I think she was also the assistant director. She said, "We're interested, if you would be, with your own show."

Before I took the first show, I went to see the chief, Jerry Rademaker. He wasn't too fond of me anyway because I had almost gotten into a physical confrontation with him at a party. When I asked if I could do the show, he said, "Aren't you the guy who grabbed me by the collar?" I said yes, it was me. He said, "You've got guts, kid, go ahead."

What had happened was I was doing a police newspaper called *The Blue Line,* and at that time there were lots of people calling police officers pigs. So I had tee shirts and sweatshirts made up with a picture of a pig wearing a police hat and under the picture, it read, "Pigs are beautiful!" We were selling them all over. People wanted them. We figured, if you're gonna call me a pig, I'll show you what a pig is. Rademaker didn't look at it that way. He was kind of angered. And I had a shirt at a party for a policeman with big medical bills or something. I had the shirt under my arm and the place was crowded and I felt somebody pull on the shirt, grab it from me and someone cussing me out. So I grabbed him by the collar. It was Rademaker and he was an inspector at the time. I said, "You touch me again, I'll knock you on your ass." Of course we were broken up. Sometime later a friend of Rademaker's who was also a friend of mine, George Washington, came over to me and said, "Rademaker asked me, 'Do you think the kid would have done it?'" I said to George, "What did you say?" He said, "I told him, 'yeah', you would." I said, "I would, too. What the hell. What could they do? Bust me lower than a patrolman?"

The radio show worked out. It was in the evening. Saturday nights for four-and-a-half hours. A talk show. That's a lot of talk. They paid me $39 per show. It was fun at times. It was a lot of work at times. It was something new. You know what the name of the show was? We called it, "Buzz the Fuzz." That was kind of controversial right away, but I figured it was the way you do these things. You kind of neutralize their venom. People would call all night long. Some of the callers were pretty smart. We had nasty ones, we had funny ones, we had a lot of different things. I had guests on my show. John Glenn when he was running for the Senate. Jim Carney when he was running for mayor of Cleveland. When I would take a break, I'd say, "Here's the weather," and I'd have my kids read the weather report. They were 8 and 10 years old. The show ran for almost two years until WERE changed its format.

HERMAN SCHMALTZ

Patrol Officer, Second District (retired)

You know, after you've been around, you experience, I don't know what it is, but you can tell the difference between a person that's drunk, under the influence, or something else. The color of his skin, you can tell. If they're slumped over the wheel of his car, you can smell alcohol. We came across a guy, he was sitting behind the wheel of his car. Anyway, we sent him to the hospital. Here, he had a diabetic, an insulin, attack. So we got a commendation and a thank you from his family and the chief. So, you know, if he's out there staggering around, maybe he's not drunk. Maybe he's sick. They grabbed his tongue and held his tongue. And I hollered to get him a bottle of soda and we trickled it down, or a candy bar, or something, and he came right out of it.

* * *

I believe in those days the policemen [got] more respect than today. Although, I've got to admit, a lot of those problems lie in the police department, too; the policemen themselves. If you go up to a citizen and say, "Hey, you, come here," or swear at them, you start off on the wrong foot.

I had one man on East 55th Street, an African American. He was 82 years old. He was involved in a little accident. I got a driver's license. I said, "Mr. Jones, what happened?" He looks and me and says, "Oh, wow." He was quiet. I said, "What's the matter, are you hurt?" He said, "I'm 82 years old, and that's the first time anybody's called me mister." He said, "Even my own kind never calls me mister." So, you know, that's the way I wanted to treat people. Like I said, I never even thought differently.

MICHAEL DUGAN

Captain (retired), Cleveland; Chief of Police, Independence

We were going somewhere, around 1985, I believe it was. It was probably six months before my promotion to lieutenant. I was a sergeant in the Third. I call this the high rate of irony. Two officers

I had got a call on an abandoned vehicle behind Sam's Pawn Shop on 29th and Prospect.

When they got there, I heard a call—I was their supervisor, a sergeant—"Get us a boss. We got a dead body in the car." While I'm en route, the second call says, "Make that two dead bodies." We get there. We hold down the crime scene. Homicide comes out. They start an investigation.

We all exchanged words about how bad crime was at 29th and Prospect, only to find out later when homicide solved the case that the murder occurred five doors away from my home in Seven Hills, and one of the murderers lived maybe two or three doors away from one of the officers on the zone car in the area of West 130th Street in Parma.

These guys went there to buy drugs. They went in the house. These guys did a robbery. They took the money. One kid was from Brecksville. They were pretty screwed up. They had been stabbed, I think, shot and it looked like somebody hit them on the head with a hatchet. The bodies were packed in the one guy's little Mustang and put behind Sam's on Prospect. We got there and we were saying, "Boy, it's getting bad around here." Then we found out that the thing happened just doors away from me.

MIKE FRICK
Sergeant, Second District (retired)

I used to get a couple bags of candy at Dean's Supply on Euclid Avenue, I used to stop there and get the bags of busted candy. Hard candy and stuff and I used to put them in a bag in the car and you'd roll up in front of a school and these kids would come over and start talking to you. You'd give them a couple pieces of candy. Or we used to get these little tiny plastic helicopters. We'd give it out to one and the next day you'd come back and you'd have three kids. Next day you'd have 25. Working day shift, if it was a little slow, you'd just hand out candy.

Back then it wasn't called PR; it was just sucking up.

Like with the whores. I've always liked to treat people the way I like to be treated. We used to deal with prostitutes all the time. The guys looked at these prostitutes like they're dirtbags. Well, some of them are, some of them aren't. Some of them are just trying to feed their families. I'm not saying it's legal or should be legalized, but I always treated them decently. If I arrested a prostitute and she wanted a cigarette, I'd give them cigarettes if I was smoking. There were many times when they were hungry so you took them over to McDonalds. You got fed for free at McDonald's sometimes, or Burger King, so you'd get them a hamburger and Coke and the next thing you know, it turns out if you were looking for a suspect, they'd help you, or it they knew something, because they were one of the best sources for information.

There was an example at the Holiday Inn on East 21st Street and Prospect Avenue. We used to have an agreement with the prostitutes because we had several guys from the Impact Unit part-timing there. As long as the prostitutes didn't go on the floors, they could come in after three or four in the morning and sit down and have coffee in the restaurant. The cooks left us big submarine sandwiches. We'd cut up the sandwiches and give them to the prostitutes. We never had any problem with them walking the floors. They'd come in and get warm when it was cold.

One night a little prostitute comes in. Her name was Cat. That was her street name. She came in and told us the place was going to get robbed. She explained to us who was going to rob it, how they were going to do it. We set it up to have extra policemen there and sure enough, these guys come in and one of them ended up getting killed. The other guy was captured. That was the kind of relationship you would get with some of the street people.

ROBERT CERBA
Lieutenant, Fraternal Order of Police

I've arrested people over the years for just being drunk in public, all the way up to homicide. I try to treat everybody like I'd want to be treated in the same situation. You have to have integrity on this job. You have to back up what you say. If I tell somebody that they're going to jail, they're going to jail. If I tell somebody that they're not going to jail, then they're not going to jail. If I promise somebody that I'm going to charge them with something, I follow through with what I promised. You have to in order to be an effective police officer. You have to be able to do your job to the best of your ability.

You have to go into court, testify as to what you saw. And 15 years now being a police officer, out of a couple hundred felony cases I've lost one felony case in a trial.

* * *

If the question is who's more dangerous, politicians or criminals, I'm going to mark them equal. And with politicians, sometimes through no fault of their own, they make decisions that af-

> **If the question is who's more dangerous, politicians or criminals, I'm going to mark them equal.**

fect the police. Politicians who think they know our job. But none of them has walked a mile in my shoes. None of them has gone out there and done this job.

In order to effectively manage somebody, you have to know what their job is. You have to be able to do their job. You have to understand their job. Councilmen are considered part-time employees. They don't want to go out. It's too much bother. There are no requirements that they be exclusively council members for the city. And a lot of them don't want to be bothered. We're necessary people. If they could find a way to do away with us, we'd be gone in a heartbeat . . . We had numerous incidents of politicians doing things that make our job and our life that much harder.

The court overtime story is a good example. Officers are the ones who are caught in the mix here. If we receive a subpoena, on every subpoena it says, "Under the penalty of law you shall not fail to show up in court, or you could be held in contempt of court." So if an officer gets a subpoena and doesn't go, and we get a judge with the wild hair, the officer could be held in contempt of court and locked up. And we've already had judges that have threatened to do that.

I don't expect the newspaper to print the whole truth, because if they find out they were wrong, they don't want to admit they were wrong. I've been the victim of some of that. I've gone out on a scene and given statements to reporters. And you see it in the newspaper or you see it on TV later—because after all the editing and the cutting and the pasting and the moving things around, it was nothing like I actually said. I've been called on the carpet by a commander and a chief because of something I said in the news media, and it was taken out of context. They edit, cut and paste things, and it sounds like I'm saying something totally different.

GREG BAEPPLER
Commander, Second District (retired)

I had my job saved by President Reagan. It was during the 1980 presidential debates. It was a zoo. You had to have motorcades and motorcycle protection to secure the streets. There's a lead car. There's two limousines, one for Reagan, and the Secret Service and SWAT and motorcycles on the side. Then an ambulance. Then maybe a bus with the press corps.

They move the principal back and forth between two limousines to confuse potential assassins. So anyway, we get everyone in. Reagan is inside. And guys loved working for Reagan. His code name was Rawhide. They're all lined up and now we got about a half hour break before Reagan leaves and goes to whatever is next.

One of my motorcycle officers leaves and heads down West Third Street toward the Justice Center. At Frankfort Avenue, some lady pulls out right in front of him. She didn't see the bike. He sees her. He sets the bike down and smacks into it. I think he might have gotten a small fracture of the arm or leg or something. Not life-threatening. In any event, my policeman's down and he's hurt. I have an ambulance 250 feet away. So I go over and tell this nice young kid from EMS. I said, "Get over there. My policeman's hurt. We gotta go."

There's this Secret Service guy in the ambulance and another technician in the back. And the kid said, "No, we can't leave the motorcade." I said, "Well, you can't, but I can," and I yanked the guy out of the ambulance. I was in uniform and I was in a real bad mood when he told me I couldn't have this ambulance for my policeman. It wasn't my intention, but he went down on the ground when I yanked him out.

For whatever reason, the Secret Service guy jumped out of the right side. This to me is a green light. I ordered a policeman to take the ambulance and pick up the injured officer. And they went to Lutheran Hospital, but in the meantime, this became the biggest deal because the president didn't have an ambulance.

I'm in trouble. I knew I was in trouble shortly after I did it. The way it was explained to me by the Secret Service guy was Reagan was perceptive enough and asked, "What's going on?" He was standing for photographs and he could tell something was going on. And he was told, "Well they took your ambulance out of the motorcade." When he gave a quizzical look, the guy said, "We had to go pick up an injured policeman," and Reagan said, "Well, that's good. That's what I would want them to do."

It probably wasn't the right thing to do, but I got away with it because Reagan said, "That's good." He wanted to know how the policeman was and he did check up on him.

MARGARET DORAN
Patrol Officer, Mounted Unit

On one of President Clinton's visits to Cleveland, I was part of the police motorcade. I had seen the pictures that the motorcycle guys had from previous motorcades. The president would get out of the limo, he'd walk down the line and shake the hands of all the dignitaries and all the police officers who were in the motorcade. A White House photographer would take pictures of each officer shaking the hand of the president. And they sent us autographed copies of the officer and the president.

And I thought, "This is one I'm going to give to my mother." As the president is working his way down the line, shaking the hands of the police officers and the dignitaries, officer John Collins is right next to me and he pokes me and says, "I'm going to tell the president that you want to kiss him. I said, "Oh, my God, John Collins, don't do that. We're both gonna be in deep shit." He said, "I don't give a damn. I'm retiring in two weeks. What do you think of that?"

So I had no idea he was really going to go through with it. Clinton shakes John's hand. He gets down to me. And I have pictures from the White House. I also have film footage from CNN. All right? I'm in the middle of shaking the president's hand. I actually had my mouth closed. Collins is between the two of us and he's got that leprechaun look on his face. And he's telling Bill Clinton, "Mr. President, she wants to kiss you." Clinton backs up. I got him by the hand. He says, "Oh my, officer, is that true?" I said, "Yes, Mr. President. I'm very Irish. And I'm sorry, this handshake business is not enough. If you hold still, this won't hurt at all."

And my recollection is, I put my left hand on the right side of his face, and I leaned up and I kissed him on the left side of his face. I got pictures back from the White House. I actually had my hand on the back of his neck, like I had him in a stranglehold. And I had him by the back of the neck and I'm kissing him on the cheek.

So Clinton backs up and I back up and we're both laughing. He says, "Officer, we don't have anything like you back in Arkansas. And I think I'd like to be arrested by you." I looked up and he's got a little smear of my lipstick on the side of his face. I started to reach up with my thumb, like your mother used to do when your face got dirty. And I thought, "If I touch this guy again, they have several Secret Service agents with large weapons."

I looked at him and I said, "Mr. President, I believe I left a little bit of lipstick on your face. I'm really sorry about that." He says, "Don't you worry about a thing, little lady, I'm going to wear it with a smile," and away goes the president of the United States with my lipstick on his face.

Unbeknownst to me, they're filming. It made CNN, the national

---

"Officer Doran. Are you the police officer I saw on CNN kissing the president of the United States?"

---

nightly news. So my lieutenant didn't talk to me for two weeks. And when he did, he could not stop hollering.

Three days later, I ran into the chief, who is now retired. And I thought I saw him before he saw me. I got really little and I tried to get away. But I heard his voice, "Officer Doran. Are you the police officer I saw on CNN kissing the president of the United States?" I went right up to him and said, "Who, me?" He said, "You know you did it." I said, "And you know I did it, too. So what's the question here? The Cleveland Police made the national nightly news. We didn't brutalize anybody. They didn't discover a drug ring operating within the police department." I said, "It was a nice public relations piece that went nationwide about Cleveland, Ohio. You shouldn't be chewing my ass. You should be giving me a commendation."

And I turned around and I started walking away. And to the back of my head, the chief says, "Margaret, you have big balls." And I turned around and I said, "Yes, I do. And they're brass and they clang when I walk."

8.

"Some stories you never want to talk about."

[KIDS IN THE CROSSFIRE]

KEVIN GRADY
Patrol Officer, Fourth District

We just got out of roll call and were working third shift. Dave Borden and I were driving down Ramona Avenue and a call came over for a domestic. We pulled up on Oakfield Avenue and saw a couple of zone cars parked there. There was a guy standing on the porch roof and he's yelling and screaming. A couple policemen are trying to settle him down and get him off the roof. He lost it during an argument with his girlfriend. And he's holding their baby in his arms. It was a four-month-old girl. The guy was either drunk or mental.

One cop goes indoors and gets the mother out. The guy moved back toward the house and reached in the window. His hand came out with a gun. He starts walking to the edge of the porch and *boom*! He's popping rounds at us. One round went right over me, and I still remember it felt like it was creasing my hair. He's using the baby as a shield, so there's no way we can return fire. The only thing you could do was haul ass and hide behind the engine block. That's your only cover.

There was a sergeant there—and this was the only funny thing that happened. It was Sergeant Harvey Romero and he's so relaxed, I think you could electrocute him and his pulse wouldn't rise. He's just a very mellow guy. The guy on the porch is popping rounds and Romero's just walking, smoking a cigarette. To this day, I don't know, that's just his personality. He's a great boss. But anyhow, that was, like I said, the only funny thing that night and the rest of it was tragic.

The guy on the porch roof is screaming and the baby is screaming. Can you imagine a gun going off next to a baby's ear? The gun fired 9 or 10 times and she was just screaming. It became a stand-off. At one point, he went back into the window and pulled out a samurai sword. He threw it at us. The blade was three-and-a-half feet long. I was pissed. I was scared, but when I get scared, I get pissed, you know what I mean?

He started pistol-whipping the baby. That's when I started feeling hatred. The feeling of helplessness was overwhelming. The guy put the baby back in the house and he came back out by himself. He had the gun in his hand. I fired two rounds at him and a few other officers fired. He went down on the roof and he was laughing. An eerie laugh.

When he went in with the baby, he had started a fire, and the fire department races over and the guy is sitting on the edge of the porch roof with the place going up in flames. We were ready

---

He started pistol-whipping the baby.
That's when I started feeling hatred.

---

to have the fire department ladder bring him down when *wham*! He jumped. He hits the walkway. The baby was with him. She bounced off the ground. He was dead. I said out loud, "You son of a bitch." I don't know what happened to the baby. One officer went to Metro to check on her and he was told, "Two broken arms, two broken legs, severe brain swelling."

Some stories you never want to talk about. This is one.

WILLIAM TELL

Commander, Sixth District (retired)

In 2001, off East 185th Street and St. Clair Avenue, there were these two kids in a field picking apples, and a guy came by with a pellet gun and shot at these two kids. Two black guys came past them and they shot these kids. The pellet killed this kid.

When I went to the hospital to see him, he was like an angel. The nicest little kid you've ever seen in your life. I think this kid was, like, 9 or 10 years old. His mother was there. The kid was an altar boy in his church. To sit there and have his parents not have anger and not have hate at those boys was the last straw for me—to see a child die so needlessly.

Two weeks prior to this, we had a situation where one of my policemen and me went into a neighborhood off of East 156th Street and Lakeshore Boulevard, and got in a car chase with some druggers. And during the car chase, he ended up in a foot chase. The policeman catches the guy and they tussle. And when they tussle, the policeman's gun goes off and it hit a kid that was standing on a tree lawn several houses away.

It was an accident, all the way. And what made me so mad was that—things start building up on me—was that black activists who did not live in that community came to that community the next day and stirred up so much trouble. They were lying about this policeman and how he had shot this kid intentionally. It was an accident. The officer was exonerated. And the ironic thing was, no one in the neighborhood was out there marching and protesting but the bad people. The good people stayed in the house because they knew what the truth was that happened out there.

These outsiders from East Cleveland came there and started trouble. This happened in 2001, in the fall. I was Sixth District commander at the time. That's what led me to saying, "I've had enough in the police department." Thirty-one years was enough for me. And I went on and retired. I had to go. That—coupled with this other kid getting killed—it was too much for me. I just saw too much violence.

BRENDA BROWN
Police Academy

In the late '80s, I was assigned to the Sex Crimes Unit. They gave me some training, but I just learned by doing. With the children, we worked hand in hand with the social workers at Metro Hospital. They would interview the kids and we would just do the follow up. Working those kind of cases did depress me. It got a to a point, I think, no one can do more than five years in that particular unit because you just get so burned out, just hearing one story after another.

I knew it was time for me to go when I was at Geauga Lake amusement park and there was this guy who was standing over his daughter and tucking her shirt into her pants. I remember looking to see how far his hand would go down the pants because you get so—you know, you just wonder.

* * *

I think the most frustrating case I had was a couple babies from the same family who had gonorrhea and there was no way to prove the case because they couldn't talk.

* * *

A 16-year-old was killed. Kidnapped, taken to an abandoned field, probably raped, and after they killed her, they tried to burn her body. The morgue called me to make the identification from a photo of the child and then tell the mother, "I don't think you want to see your child this way. You want to remember her the way she was the last time you saw her." The mother was at the morgue. I made the identification. Then I met with the mother.

HERMAN SCHMALTZ
Patrol Officer, Second District (retired)

Early one morning, it must have been around three A.M., we saw this boy—I believe he was four years old—walking down Starkweather Avenue. We called him over. He came over. We asked him where he lived. He didn't know. We asked him his name. He didn't know. So we got him in the police car. We were riding up and down the street.

Finally, somebody, I guess, was going to work. They looked and they see the little guy and they say, "Oh, that's, so and so." I said, "Well, where does he live?" He showed us. We go down there and people are still asleep.

We go banging on the door, and finally, they go, "What do you want? What do you want?" They finally come to the door and I said, "Did you lose someone?" They said, "What?" I said, "This little guy here." They say, "Oh, my God." The door opens.

There's two locks on the door. He was doing this all the time, I guess. What he was doing, the bottom line was, he got the bottom opened, then turned the chair over and got the top one opened. Then went outside and was just walking. Those days, it wasn't like today. Today, someone would grab him and take him away.

ROBERT LEGG
Lieutenant, Third District (retired)
The worst was a shooting on East 71st Street off Holton Avenue. It was the middle of day and we had shots fired. It was the mid-'80s and I was a lieutenant then. When we entered the residence, we found the bodies of a man and a woman. They had been executed, shot to death. They had a five-year-old son and the gunman took the child with him. We got a description of the vehicle and put out an all-points bulletin. We were frantic to get that kid. We went up and down every street. We didn't get him. The gunman shot the kid to death and threw his body out of the car. The gunman was caught, but not right away.

* * *

In 1972, there was a cheat spot on Grand Avenue off East 77th. It was late. Some guy inside was playing with a gun and it went off. The bullet went through the forehead of a 12-year-old girl sitting on the couch. By that time I had been on the department for

3 years and I had become so hardened, it was routine. I know that sounds crazy, but I had trained myself, whether it was brains on the ceiling or body parts, to deal with it abstractly, as I would a broken window. Not to take away from humanity, but it was a way of dealing with it, to treat it only as evidence for the sake of survival.

TAMI TONNE
Sergeant, Narcotics
We're in the projects on a drug raid. Front door and back door. Another detective and I are covering the back. I hear the banging on the front door and a half dozen guys are running out the back door. We yelled for them to get down and I couldn't believe they actually did. We got everybody settled. There were four or five kids, screaming and crying. Crack cocaine all over the place. They were bagging it and smoking it at the same time. What can you tell the little kids? They ask, "Are you taking Mommy to jail?" And we say, "We're just taking her to talk with her. You'll see her tomorrow."

JEFF STANCZYK
Patrol Officer, Third District
I think criminals used to be classier. These folks have no honor. They'll do anybody they can—kids, old people.

I have one of the saddest things, and I was not there, but I saw what it did to the policeman that was a real nice copper that's still on. It wasn't too long ago, 15 years maybe. You can look it up.

There was a call. A lady came to the door—it was a domestic violence. She was naked and bloody, and she told the policemen that were there, "He's in there with the kids." And what the guy had done—and you would remember this story—he took a knife and cut his kids' heads off and he put them on a stove, one of those old, we used to call them ghetto stoves, those old projects stoves. You could turn them up. They used to turn them up to heat their houses. And he put fire under all the kids' heads and he put the bodies in the bathtub.

The policeman that I know that went into that house came out another man. Whatever he needed to handle what he saw in that house, he left in that house. To this day, he's still on the job. It's not that he's meaner; he's different. A piece of him is still in that house. I'm telling you. And that's what people don't get. That's the

---

The policeman that went into that house came out another man. Whatever he needed to handle what he saw in that house, he left in that house. It's not that he's meaner; he's different. A piece of him is still in that house.

---

part that people don't get. They wonder why policemen throw up a wall. It's like on Star Trek, they put these shields up, but they can't beam anybody in. The wall does two things: keep things from getting in, keep things from getting out, too. And they can't shut it off when they get home.

* * *

The last call that we got when I was working in Second District, which was in 1989 . . . we got a call for a boy electrocuted on Cass Avenue, off of West 58th Street. There was an electrical generator place in there. There was a kid laying on top of this generator, or whatever the hell it was. I couldn't see what it was. And there was a crowd.

The mother was there. This woman attached herself to me. She said, "Can you tell me if my boy's alive? Can you tell me if my boy's alive?" I said, "Ma'am, I don't know."

And I had learned, many years before that, many years before . . . We had a call for a kid shot. There was a boy laying under a pine tree. He had put a rifle in his mouth, took a yardstick, pushed the trigger and he blew out his brains. EMS was there. They picked him up, threw him in the wagon. The sergeant says, "Go in and tell the family the kid's dead." We went to the hospital and, here, the kid wasn't dead. It went through here, and it flew out under his ear, and he didn't hit anything that was vital enough to kill him. It nicked this artery, but then what do you say? So I learned something from that. I'm no coroner. I'm no doctor. I pronounce nobody dead.

So the woman's on me, "Please can you tell me, just tell me if you think he's dead?" I said, "Ma'am, I honestly don't know." I said, "Come on with us, we'll take some information." We got her away. The utility workers got there, cut the power, got the kid off, threw him in the back of the EMS wagon. They took him up to St. John's—that place that used to be on Detroit Avenue. What we didn't know was, the older daughter followed the wagon there. We were getting the information, getting it from the kids, "What happened? What happened?" The kid's ball went in there. The kid climbed the fence, went up there, touched something and got shocked.

Well, we go to the hospital, because you've got to view the body. You don't know if the kid was shot, stabbed, thrown up there; you don't know. We go to the hospital, St. John's, and pulled the sheet back there. It's a kid I know from Medic Drug, where I work part-time security. Now I really feel bad.

When the electricity went in, it went in his arm, and it blew out the side of his face. That kid was in heaven before he knew what was going on. Electricity has to leave your body somewhere, and that's what it did. That kid was . . . there was no blood because he was cooked.

Now we've got to go back and tell the mother. What we didn't know was that the daughter had already left and went back to the house on Herman Avenue. We pull up and knock on the door. The lady comes to the door. I said, "Ma'am, on behalf of the . . ." And she slapped me across the face. She goes, "This is what I'm going to tell you. You gave me false hope about my son. I know he's dead. He was dead on that electrical whatever." She goes, "I'll never forget that." She slammed the door in my face.

That woman comes up to Medic to this day, and she won't say a word to me. She won't say a word. And she knows I work Fridays. And I'll see her, maybe, once a year. She won't say a word to me. And that's the way it is.

* * *

We got a call for domestic violence in that big battleship on West 25th Street and Bridge Avenue. A lady comes to the door and says, "Oh, my boyfriend's in there with the baby."

And it's one of the few times this has happened to me. What I saw, I stepped out of myself and watched myself watch what was going on and everything slowed down. It was like, remember those old kaleidoscope machines, remember? Where you take the crank and it would flip the pictures, the old ones? And the quicker you cranked it, the more it looked like the people were moving?

We walked in that room, and there was about a two- or three-year-old kid standing in a crib performing oral sex on this guy, and the guy had a gun in his hand. He was standing by the window, and I just fell out of myself. I saw me, my partner and this guy, covering this guy, yelling. It was like everything was slow. And they say, your mind slows stuff down so you can react to it. And it happened to me, I'm telling you, twice. I looked. It was like something out of a movie. The kid didn't know. He was sucking this guy's crank, and the guy had a gun in his hand. And he looked at us and he threw the gun out the window.

And my partner, I remember him telling me, "We should just dust this guy right here." And we didn't. I tell the people in my class, if you think you would've shot that guy, then don't take this job on. Because it ain't my job to execute people. We could've said, "Hey, listen, the guy had a gun in his hand, he was out the window, he went to raise it, and we shot him and killed him." There wouldn't have been no problem.

JOE SADIE
Captain, Cops for Kids Program

I went into a house where the lady who lived there got pistol-whipped. We did a thing on Christmas morning with a local television station and reporter. The little boy thought Santa wasn't coming because he was poor, because grandma couldn't afford to buy him any gifts.

A guy named Peters out in the Sixth District, Detective Peters, did the report. She was pistol-whipped and robbed. Now what they could've robbed from her, I don't know. He told me the story. He said, "Captain, how about we do Christmas for this kid?" But I never do it on Christmas morning, because by then, I've done all my sites and I spend it with my family.

But I went out on this Christmas morning. I went into the house in uniform, and there's this little boy. He was a little black kid who couldn't have weighed more than 30 pounds. He was no bigger than a couple phone books. And I just started talking to him. Grandma was there. She knew we were going to help him.

I asked him where his gifts were. He said, "Santa isn't coming this year because we don't have any money. We got robbed." I said, "Are you sure about that? Santa doesn't skip the good little boys."

So I picked up my cell phone and I made a phone call to Santa Claus who, of course, was standing outside the door. I said, "I'll have Santa Claus brought here by the police. We don't let little kids go through Christmas without any presents." So within a minute, because the cameras were rolling, there was a knock on the door because Santa Claus was out there. And let me tell you, remember the commercial, "priceless?" This kid's face was priceless.

KEVIN GRADY
Patrol Officer, Fourth District

The first time I saw this kid it was the middle of the night. We saw him at East 143rd Street and Spear Avenue. He was maybe 5 feet tall, 70 pounds soaking wet. He was obviously breaking curfew.

It turned out he was 16. We started talking to him and the kid started spitting out rocks of crack cocaine. He had so many rocks in his mouth, he couldn't talk. So he started spitting them out by accident. That was probably the easiest drug arrest we ever made. He seemed like a decent kid. He was fairly polite. He was new to this. We took him to Detention Home, but they wouldn't take him because they said the kid didn't have enough felonies on him. So we took him back to where we first found him.

Along the way, we tried to tell him he was in the wrong business, that the guys in the drug business are bad guys, mean guys, and that he'll get hurt. He wasn't cut out to be a dealer. I told him

---

He wasn't cut out to be a dealer. I told him drugs were not the career he wanted. Three months later he was shot to death.

---

drugs were not the career he wanted. Three months later he was shot to death. His body was found just a few blocks from where we met and talked with him.

KEITH HAVEN
Sergeant, Strike Force, First District

My partner, Joe Cavanaugh, and I were walking into the district. This was sometime in the '90s. I think it was a little rainy that night, a dreary kind of night. It was 11 o'clock at night and we were walking into the district. We got off duty at 11:30, I think. And we hear just an incredible car crash in front of the district. We literally dropped everything we had. We could tell it was a pretty severe crash.

We go running out there and there's a car flipped on its side. And there's another car several hundred feet down West 130th. This is right at West 130th and West Avenue. And the car's on its side. I climbed to the top of the car. I'm literally laying on the driver's side of the car, in the car. And there's an elderly lady that basically had her head split open by a fire hydrant. The car tipped on its side, tipped the fire hydrant, and it ripped open part of her head.

The driver of the car was awake and talking to me, but dying while I was holding onto her. This was her daughter, and she was probably in her 30s, and her children were in back and they were all okay, so they could all see what was going on. Grandma died. Mom died in my arms waiting for the fire department, and the kids sat there and watched them.

And the driver of the [other] car was drunk. After the fire department got the kids out and they got away from the car, and they're walking him to another car, he said, "I didn't do anything wrong."

It was one of those days when it just takes everything you got and just takes it out of you. I was so drained, I had to sit down. I couldn't even stand up. I walked inside and sat down. I probably sat there for half an hour, 40 minutes, before I could even get up and go change clothes. It was a terrible, horrific thing to see. I'd have to guess this was '95 or '96. It was a little bit cool outside. The youngest children were very small. I don't know if they were strapped in or not. It was a station wagon. They had to break the back window to get them out. They took them out the back of the car. That was bad.

KEVIN GRADY
Patrol Officer, Fourth District

I was on the job about three months, afternoon shift, springtime. We got a Code 3 from an intoxicated female having husband trouble. Calls like that are very, very common. When we get to the scene, the woman tells us she's tired of hooking for dope. Turns out she was a prostitute for dope and her old man is cooking up the stuff in the kitchen and he's with the dealers.

We go in the house and find the woman's sister sitting, dead drunk, by the door, and the husband is mad because his wife doesn't want to hook anymore for dope.

This would have been a routine assignment except there were two kids in there, too. One about five and the other about seven. Beautiful kids. They were sitting, hands folded, quiet, they looked like a couple of parochial school kids in a class. I went over and talked to the kids. They were very, very bright kids. Lieutenant Walter May was there and he's looking and he tells one of the officers, "Go up and get these kids something to eat."

There wasn't any food in the house. He took money out of his pocket and said, "Get them Happy Meals." I always thought that was kind of ironic. Happy Meals. Beautiful kids. Horrible home. We took the kids out of the home, of course. I often wonder how they turned out. It's calls like that that will punch you right in the heart, I don't care how tough you are.

PAUL FALZONE
Detective, Sixth District

With missing kids, some policemen, including myself, would take their own cars back after the shift and continue looking. Byrl Holbert and I looked all night long for a kid once. A little 6-year-old girl. It was 1970 and late in the fall because we looked at each other and said, "We've got find this kid." Byrl was an older guy. He had me by six years on the job, at least. He was a very diligent worker, one of the hardest workers I worked with. It got to be 4:30

I always thought that was kind of ironic. Happy Meals. Beautiful kids. Horrible home.

---

in the morning and Byrl said, "Let's stop the car and think." We pulled into a McDonald's. I said, "Byrl, I'm so tired I think I'm seeing things. I just saw two rats come out from underneath the fence over there. Those rats were as big as dogs. They're probably going in the garbage. But if you look real close, it looks like there's a little pair of tennis shoes under the thing." We got out of the car, opened the gate and looked in there. The little girl was inside. Sleeping. We took the kid home. That's what policemen do. That's what it's all about.

JEFF STANCZYK
Patrol Officer, Third District

We got a call, down off of West 25th, and it was a hot, hot summer day. The call was for a strange odor coming from an apartment. We walked up. The door was open. There was a lady rocking in a chair, a young girl. An Appalachian girl. What we had found out was, her husband went hunting and she had been home alone. Apparently, they had a baby, and apparently, the baby had died. The woman found the kid and freaked out and was rocking with this kid, trying to breast-feed this dead baby. And the kid had been like that for three days. He was, like, swollen, and his skin was splitting already. You know, when the body gets hot. And she was singing, "Daisy," to this little baby. We're sitting there and we're talking to her. She didn't want to come with us. We said, "You know, you gotta come with us." Then we said, "You know, your baby needs to go to the hospital to be seen. He's not looking very well." And she got up. She didn't want the baby in the backseat of the cruiser. So we put her in the backseat and I held the baby while she was back there. She was singing to the kid the whole time. It's like something out of a book.

BOB TONNE
Detective, Robbery (retired)

Me and my partner were cruising down Woodland Avenue. We passed East 89th Street, this big apartment house and we looked over to the side and we saw a blaze back there, a fire. So we went off the roadway and came back, and Holy Christ, it was a fire! I mean, it was blazing. So we ran out, and some guy on the second floor jumped out and landed and broke his leg. We went to the back and there's 12 kids up on the second floor balcony. We told them to jump and we caught them, one at a time, as they jumped out. Me and my partner were holding our hands together and we got all of them. There was one who was pretty big, too. My partner got a sore back out of it, but we did pretty good. And what happened, the woman who set the fire poured gasoline all the way up the steps. She set it on fire and that was the only way out of that apartment. Four or five kids died. They convicted her of murder.

KYLE STOUGES
Patrol Officer, Third District

There was a female on West 73rd Street, close to Clark Avenue. She felt suicidal and she didn't want to hurt her kids, so she called us. When we responded, it was a wonderful house, a well-kept place. It's pretty bad down there. It was as if someone took a nice suburban house and dropped it in the middle of Shit Town, USA.

But she had three wonderful kids, a baby, a 7-year-old, and an 11-year-old. And her husband just picked up and left. She didn't have family in the area, and she didn't want to hurt her kids, so she wanted help.

We called the boss on the scene. It was Christmas time, 1999. We tracked down her mom. Mom lived in Vermilion and was all upset because she couldn't get a car to come out and pick up the children. When the lieutenant arrived, I explained the situation to him and said, "I know it's a lot to ask, but let me and my partner drive these kids out to Vermilion."

The kids were obviously close. While we were there, the oldest is holding his baby brother and the other one was showing us colored pictures. I said, "We can't have them spending Christmas Eve in Child Services. Mom's going to get some help and she'll probably get released eventually." So he approved it.

I think it was the first time I've heard of a baby seat getting strapped in the backseat of a zone car. We got the baby all bundled up, put him in the baby seat, strapped them all in. We opened the sliding partition and I said, "All right, we're headed to your grandma's house in Vermilion." The baby fell asleep. We get out there, and the look on grandma's face . . . she was beyond words. I have to tell you, that was the best I ever felt helping children.

DANNY CONNORS
Patrol Officer, First District

I used to be into stolen cars. I led the city in stolen car arrests for a couple of years. We had just come from a gun run, where somebody was threatening with a gun. That scene was all cleared up and we're driving northbound on East 131st Street.

At Ferris Avenue, there's a van sitting there waiting to go into the intersection. The driver looked at me and he had this look on his face, it was like, "Holy shit, it's the police!" So I look at him and I look at the car. I see the door lock hanging from the hole where it's supposed to be, so I knew it was just punched. I told my partner to run the plate. It belonged to some Polish guy who didn't even live in Cleveland, and the driver sure wasn't Polish. So it's gotta be stolen. We start after him.

There were about 10 cars between us. He cut left of center, through a red light, clipped a car and heads down East 131st Street. We immediately turn on the lights and sirens to get through traffic. I'm thinking he's going to turn a corner and bail. The good car thieves know that. The longer you stay in a chase, the more likely you are to get caught. We were still about two blocks back when he's driving down East 128th Street, getting close to Beachwood Avenue and he takes a left. I tell my partner, "Okay, get ready, he's gonna bail." He doesn't bail.

We get on to Beachwood, he's still going. He's approaching East 131st Street and he's not slowing down at all. All of a sudden he hits the intersection. A car's coming through and—BAM!—he hits it. The car goes flying into a front porch on the opposite side of the street.

We finally get up there and the guy is bailing and running. Other cars are coming to assist us and we ended up catching him in the backyard. Police officers are already helping the people in the other car. Well, it turns out one was a six-year old girl. She didn't make it. She got killed. She didn't die right away. She got taken to the hospital and I felt really bad. I wanted to strangle the guy. I mean, I had a six-year old girl at the time. That could have been my wife driving down the street and that happened. I'm wondering if it's my fault. I'm just doing my job. I didn't want this to happen. Why didn't he stop? Why didn't he jump out? He should have jumped out. He had every opportunity to jump out. We weren't even close to him.

EMS came and took the little girl to Rainbow Babies & Children's Hospital and took her mother to another hospital. Like I said, I wanted to strangle that guy. I couldn't believe what he did. I said to him, "Look what you did to this little girl. She's hurt and you'd better hope to God she makes it."

I'm praying the whole time, "God, take care of her. Don't let her be seriously hurt." I went to the hospital and I'm getting evil eyes from all the doctors and nurses. They thought I chased the woman's car and killed the little girl. Doctors pulled me into a room and said to me, "What were you doing? How could you?" I said, "I wasn't chasing her. There was another car and I was catching up to the car. You can say I was chasing it, you can also say I wasn't. I wasn't close enough to get to the car. He initiated the pursuit by going across center and hitting a car."

One of the doctors told me she wasn't going to make it. I talked to the grandfather of the child and I told him that I was sorry and I told him what had happened and I said the prayers that I can offer from my family and my church would be with his granddaughter and his daughter. I said, "I'm sorry this happened." I gave him a hug and I left. I went home and prayed.

I stopped looking for stolen cars.

9.

"I'm trying not to laugh . . ."

[COP HUMOR]

ED KOVACIC
Chief (retired)

When I was with the decoy squad, we got a complaint on the West Side, around West 25th Street and Broadview Road. Some kid was grabbing women. A male would run up behind these women and grab their breasts from behind. They had a description that went anywhere from 14 to 40 and anywhere from 5 foot 6 to 6 foot tall. This was 1964.

We said it was the paperboy. Always the same time of day. But the argument came back, "What about the description?" Well, these women didn't know what they were seeing when they were grabbed like that.

Our decoys carried radios, but for some reason they weren't allowed to talk over them, only signal. They had earpieces so we could say, "Bill, are you okay?" You'd hear a squelch. One squelch was yes, two was no, and when he got into trouble he just kept hitting the button; then you knew.

Bill Margo was a good looking guy, but when he'd dress up as a woman, he made a real nice looking woman. We set up on two sides of a church. Two decoys were out walking around, and we sat in the cars, waiting.

At six in the morning, Bill's signaling trouble and we ran across the street into a parking lot and found his purse, but no Bill. We spread out looking for him. I found him. He was walking through yards. One of his heels was broken. The wig was twisted around sideways on his head. His blouse was pulled open and the rags that were used to stuff his brassiere were hanging out. Imagine him walking with a broken heel.

I said, "Bill, are you okay?" He said, "Those fucking West Side drivers, those sons of bitches!" I said, "What are you talking about?" He said, "You were right. It's the paperboy. I chased him down the street, the little shit, and he got away and ran. I went out on the street and I tried to flag down a car." Now imagine, he's got the wig on sideways, his blouse got torn open and the rags are hanging out of his bra. And he said, "So I held up my badge and they just passed me by! None of them stopped! So I figured if I held up my gun, they'd stop. They went left of center! They went around me!"

I was laughing. I said, "How the hell did he get away from you?" He said, "Well, Jesus Christ, we were told he was going to come up from behind and grab us by our boobs. He went up under my dress, grabbed me by the balls and started squeezing. Jeez, I couldn't do anything. Then he started running."

We get back and find everybody else and we see this kid walking down the street delivering papers. Bill said, "That's not him." We went over and grabbed this kid. He said, "It's the regular paperboy. I just help him out. He's my friend. He does this. He's the one that does this, grabbing women." He told us where this kid lived.

We went over and the parents were Jehovah's Witnesses and they told the kid not to lie. So the kid admitted it. We told the parents we were going to take him downtown, book him, and bring him back. So we get this kid in the car and we said, "How come when you grabbed the other women, you always grabbed them around the top and grabbed their breasts?"

He said, "I wanted to know what it felt like. That's why I did it. I wanted to know what it felt like." So I said, "Well why did you go up and grab under the dress this time?" He said, "Well, I wanted to see what the difference was, if there was a difference between men and women." I couldn't help it. I said, "Well, was there a difference?" He said, "Not that I could tell."

EDDIE MCGOUN
Detective

It was my first experience with computers. It was mid-'60s, I guess, and I was working the computer on the third floor of old Central Station. Frank Corrigan and Lenny Malloy came up to look at it. I had been in the academy with Lenny, and Frank and I used to be partners. They were looking for an armed robber. Black guy.

So I'm telling them that the computer, fed the right information, would produce the name of the suspect, if he was there. So they're giving me the information and I'm punching it in and then I said, okay, boys, get ready, because in just a minute or two, your suspect's name is going to appear.

Who appears? Louis Finklestein, an old Jewish guy whose nickname was, 'Louie the Dip,' because he was a pickpocket. He was the wrong age, wrong color and had never been known to use a gun. So much for high-tech.

KEITH HAVEN
Sergeant, Strike Force, First District

It's one minute to the next, one day to the next. You can leave work laughing about something that happened, and the next day you can leave work completely emotionally drained. It just takes a lot out of you . . .

While I was on probation, one of my training officers, who I won't mention, was telling me all these jokes, and we got a call for this guy who was dead. EMS was there and checked him. I can't tell you what street it was. It's off West 117th. It was warm. It was springtime, probably May of '95. Maybe April. But, he's telling me these jokes, and we get there and we're in the house with the family and the friends of this guy. And we obviously had to check the body and make sure there was no foul play or anything.

The guy had been taking a lot of medication—depressants and stuff like that, narcotic-type drugs for whatever illness he had, and he drank a lot the night before. It didn't work out well, obviously. And when the body lays a certain way, there's marbling on the skin because the way the blood and fluid settles in the body. This gentleman had died on his face, like, laying face down. So we turned him over. The whole side of his face was marbled. It looks like marble. It's purplish, reddish swirls, and it looked like he had been beaten or something.

That's what the family thought. They're going ballistic thinking somebody beat him. We're trying to calm them down. We had just gotten them calmed down and my training officer says something that triggers this joke. So now I'm fighting with every strength that I have. I'm trying to be decent with the family and not act like a complete moron, but I'm trying not to laugh.

> **So I have to go back in the room with the dead guy and close the door because I'm laughing so hard.**

So I have to go back in the room with the dead guy and close the door because I'm laughing so hard. And I had to stay in there for a couple minutes with this dead body, and acting like I had to check the body.

He did it on purpose and he got me good.

CHESTER TORBINSKI
Lieutenant, Accident Investigation Unit

In the early '60s, we were driving down Euclid Avenue and the next thing you hear, *crash!*, like glass being shattered. I looked down. There's a guy standing in front of a shoe store. I don't remember the name of it. He's just standing there.

I said, "Hey, what's going on?" He said, "Oh, I just don't feel good. I had too much to drink, and took a rock and broke this window." So we called the zone car. And they knew the guy. The zone guy said, "Oh, yeah. He's a homeless." We didn't have too many of them, but we still had them. They said, "Well, take care of him. We'll just throw them in the can." I said, "Okay."

And lo and behold, I'm in court the next day. I recognized this guy in front of the judge. And he makes a big speech when he was sentencing him. He said, "I'm not going to put up with this kind of behavior if you can't hold your drinks," and goes through this big spiel. He says, "For your sentence you get 90 days in the work house."

The guy says, "Thank you, Your Honor," and they hauled him off. People in the courtroom were like, "Wow! Did you hear that? 90 days!" They were all excited. They were worried about *their* cases.

So, I come to work that night, and I'm telling the zone car, I said, "You know what? The guy got 90 days for that." They said, "Yeah, well, you know, it's going to be winter time. And that's what they do. They break the window, commit a crime, then they go to the work house. They have a place for the winter." That was just a ploy by the judge. He felt sorry for them . . . Like I say, you live and learn. There's good people in this world.

TOM ARUNSKI
Patrol Officer, Third District (retired)

I'm working the wagon with this old-timer. He had fought in the Battle of the Bulge. He was a paratrooper, one of those World War II guys. He always drove. I swear he couldn't read or write because I made out all the reports. That was no big deal because I was learning and I didn't really care one way or another.

One day we get an OB call, a woman having a baby. It was down an alleyway off Payne Avenue. We go up and take our OB kit with us. There's a Puerto Rican family up there and they spoke very little English. Once we get in, sure enough, she's having a baby. I mean, there's no putting her on a stretcher. She's having the baby.

My partner says, "I'm not doing this. You put on the gloves and you do it."

There was nothing to it. You open up the OB kit and it's got everything written out. What you're supposed to do and what you're not supposed to do. Stuff like that. It was no big deal. I pulled the baby out and cut the cord.

So we're taking the mother and the baby and the family members over to Metro Hospital. And my partner's yelling, "Yeah, Arunski delivered it!" So we're walking out of the hospital and the old man—I'm assuming it was the father—said, "What's your name?" And I said, "Arunski," and he said, "How do you spell it?" And I spelled it for him. I thought he was going to make a complaint against me, but he said, "I'm going to name the baby after you."

So my partner and I are walking out and he says to me, "If they call that kid Arunski Gonzales, do you realize how tough that kid's going to be?"

ALAN CIELEC
Patrol Officer, First District (retired)
My partner was Eddie Bendzik. We called him "Cementhead." He and I were sitting at West 104th Street and Lake Avenue; only had a half hour left on our shift. We're facing south and watching the cars come off the Shoreway.

There's a streetlight above us and it lights up the police car. So Eddie takes his flashlight and says, "Watch this." He turns it on and points it at the streetlight. The light sensor inside the streetlight then thinks it's daylight and the light goes off. It would stay off for about five minutes. Then Eddie would do it again.

A Corvette came flying through the red light, then through another red light at West 110th Street. We pulled her over. Her license plate was ELEVEN. I shouldn't have gone to the driver alone, but I did. I said, "Don't worry, I'll get out."

There was a guy, kind of slumped, in the passenger seat. I looked at the girl and she's got this blouse on that's half unbuttoned and nothing underneath. My flashlight started shaking in my hand. So I asked her for her driver's license. She said, "What did I do wrong?" Well, with me, that's two tickets right there. When they ask me a question like that and they know what they did. I said, "You don't know what you did wrong?" She knows. So I said, "Is this your current address? What's your phone number? What year is your car?" I said, "Hang on, I'll be right back."

So I go back to the car and say, "Eddie, you gotta see this. You gotta see this girl. You gotta see this. Eddie, you gotta see this girl." So Eddie comes out with his flashlight to the passenger side. He doesn't have the view I have. And this time the blouse is all unbuttoned and open. My flashlight's really shaking and this dirtbag in the other seat is still passed out.

Turned out she was 35 and he was 30. Looked like drugs to me. And I'm looking at my watch and we have to get out of there, so I said, "Hon, I'm gonna let you go. I'm just gonna let you go, just be more careful." Well, I did say, "We just got a radio assignment we have to cover." And then I said, "But I gotta know something." She said, "What?" I said, "Your license plate, ELEVEN, what does that stand for?" She looked at me and said, "Sweetheart, on a scale from 1 to 10, I'm an 11."

EMIL CIELEC
Patrol Officer, Accident Investigation Unit

When I was a young cop on the West Side, we got a call about a missing kid. Me and my partner went to the house and banged on the door, but nobody answered. We walked around back and there's the mother of this missing kid, smoking a cigarette and talking with her boyfriend. I said, "Why aren't you looking for your kid?" and she said, "That's your job."

We looked all day but didn't find him. Toward the end of the shift, we get a call from a woman about 20 blocks away who found this little boy. We go over and get him and take him home. Well, what this woman had done with him was give him a bath and clean clothes from her own kids.

When the mother saw us walking up, the kid in our arms, she looked and looked and looked at the kid and then she said, "Danny? Danny, is that you?" She ran up and pulled his lip up. He was missing a tooth and that's how she knew it was him! He was so dirty when he walked away that she didn't recognize him when he came back.

So for years after that, my partner and I would use it as sort of a funny password, "Danny? Danny, is that you?"

FRANK BOVA, SR.
Patrol Officer, Second District (retired)

In 1986, they were dredging the mouth of the river and they pulled out a car. We were right there. We ran the plates. The plate was stolen 10 years prior. All of a sudden, the water and mud were

---

The lesson from this story is always buy Hanes underwear.

---

rushing out of the car and you see part of a body in the car. But it was only the lower torso. Then we did a little more investigating and found the kid had been missing for 10 years, too. But we still don't know how he got in the river. But the lesson from this story is always buy Hanes underwear. Ten years at the bottom of the Cuyahoga and all that's left is Hanes underwear. That's all I'm getting the rest of my life.

TOM DIEMERT
Sergeant, Fifth District (retired)

We had a bank robbery at Society on Public Square in the '70s. I got the call and I headed down to Ontario from West 3rd Street and Superior Avenue. I made the turn at Public Square and for some reason my horse, Gypsy, went up in the air. That's when everybody yelled. I had drawn my gun because I'm looking for bank robbers. I have my gun in one hand, the reins in the other, and Gypsy goes up. I heard a guy say, "Hey, look! The Lone Ranger!"

MICHAEL DUGAN
Captain (retired), Cleveland; Chief of Police, Independence

Well, in 1993, an anti-abortion group had a series of demonstrations. I think they were called Operation Rescue. They held one on Carnegie Avenue, one on Chester Avenue, and a third one on Shaker Boulevard around East 117th Street. This woman walks up to one of our officers and says, "I can tell by the look in your eyes that you think that I'm worthless."

The officer replied, "No, ma'am, don't feel that way at all. This is my day off so you're not worthless, you're worth time-and-a-half to me."

* * *

Garfield Park is in Garfield Heights. It's off Broadway. But it's owned by the city of Cleveland, so Cleveland police patrol it. In the Fourth, we had an officer that screwed up everything he touched, so we thought putting him in the park would be the answer. We told him just to go to the park, watch the kids, and don't get in any trouble. His sergeant came to the swimming pool one day to check him. What the sergeant found was that the officer was swimming in the pool with his badge pinned to his swimming trunks and his gun and uniform underneath the lifeguard's chair.

MICHAEL DUGAN
Captain (retired), Cleveland; Chief of Police, Independence

When I was a rookie, I would sometimes get the mail run detail. It meant going to Central Station and picking up warrants and any mail for the district. I was brand new and I walked into the mail center and I said, "Whattya got for the Fourth District?" The old-timer's reply was, "Sympathy, kid. Sympathy."

JIM GNEW

Patrol Officer, SWAT

My first accident was also my first fatal. It was at East 55th Street and Francis Avenue. We went racing down there and the car was really messed up. I was working with these real old-timers and they told me, "Kid, go out there and do traffic."

Ten minutes later they called me, "Kid, you need to help us get him out of here." They told me to go to the passenger side door and lift his legs. They said, "We're going to pull him out nice and easy." The guy was really mangled. I remember holding his left leg and these guys are pulling the guy out. I see the guy going, but the leg ain't going nowhere. And I see the big, old smirks on their faces because they already knew the guy was dead and had his leg severed. They wanted to see the look on my face when they were holding the body and I was holding the leg.

BILLY EVANS

Detective, Auto Theft (retired)

I'll tell you, the funniest thing that ever happened to me was in the Auto Theft Unit. I had a lot of snitches who would tell me who was driving stolen cars and so on. Well, this particular guy, Elmer Washington, he left town because he knew there were warrants out for him.

So he left town and went over to Youngstown and he bought some different identification. So, they called me and told me he was driving a stolen car and he was living off of East 65th Street.

I went over there and was sitting there waiting for him hoping he would get in the car. Finally he did get in the car and I started following him. I called radio for some backup and they told me they didn't have anyone to send. I was working alone. I used to work alone a lot in the Auto Theft Unit.

So, after a while, I guess he looked in the rearview mirror and he observed me following him. So, he pulled over and bailed out and I had to chase him down. Well, finally I did get some help. So, I told the guys that I had Elmer Washington. He swore up and down that his name was *not* Elmer Washington.

So, we got into the Fourth District and he had his state identification card with some [other guy's] name out of Youngstown. We put that name on the computer with that Social Security number he had and it came up that [that guy] was wanted in Youngstown for a homicide.

When they told him that, he said, "You know who I am. You know my name's Elmer Washington." Right away he wasn't that other guy. That was the dumbest prisoner. What happened was that he bought the identification off of a woman, he said. And this woman probably knew her son was wanted, so she sold him the identification.

KYLE STOUGES
Patrol Officer, Third District

In May of 2002, we get an alarm trip at Longwood Plaza, on East 40th Street and Community College Avenue. Heavy drugs there. That's where [police officer] Wayne Leon was shot and killed. All the storefronts are gated and secured.

We went in front and didn't see anything. We drove around back. We had a guy who was hammering into the back end of the store. Going through the cinder block, hammering with a sledge-hammer. All we saw were his legs from about the thigh down.

Now the funny thing was, his shoes were missing, his socks were missing, and his pants were missing. We went up to him and I said, "Are you all right?" And he screamed, "Please get me out of here! Please get me out of here!"

So we pulled him out and he's got a couple handful of clothes. He told us, "Yeah, I was breaking in. I was trying to steal clothes." I said, "Okay, I can see that. That's evident. But where are your shoes? Your socks? And where are your pants?"

He said, "Well, I had some brand-new Nikes. Someone saw those, so they stole them off me instead of helping me. And then some other guy said, 'Man, those are good pants.' I said, 'Help me. I'll get you *three* pairs of pants,' but he said, 'That's all right, I'll just take these.'"

So I asked him, "How come you don't have any socks on?" He said, "Because when he pulled the shoes off, he just ripped them off so fast he took my socks with him."

And I thought there was honor among thieves. I guess there's not. They would roll over on their sister. You said, "Help," they'd help you, all right.

ELMER WALLING
Patrol Officer, Statement Unit (retired)

I went to Grace Hospital with two homicide detectives. This was for a victim of a shooting. He was in the back of the room. I think there were two people in the room and he was in the back. I had to go in between the two beds and I set my portable typewriter up so I could take his statement. And he had tubes in his nose and whatever. There were a lot of people talking, and every time I would ask something, I'd have to bend over the hospital bed and put my ear down by his mouth so I could understand. And he was gurgling and I couldn't understand him. Then he said that I was standing on his tubes! I was choking the poor guy to death. And I was taking the statement, so I had to keep bending over to listen to him and I put my hand on the wrong key row. And when I got done with the statement, it was all garbage!

HERMAN SCHMALTZ
Patrol Officer, Second District (retired)

Tom McGuire—he was a very devout Catholic. So we get a call from a church. There are two men dressed as nuns soliciting stuff at houses down off of Bridge Avenue. So we go over there, and yeah, they've got whiskers, hair, and everything else.

But they were women. I said, "They can't speak English. They're Italian." So we take them over to St. Rocco's on Fulton Road, and asked the priest there the question. We told him what we got them for. He's talking to them. And he said, "Yeah, they're nuns. They're from Italy. And they're staying out at the convent out there in Richfield. And they didn't know that they can't do that."

So, I said, "Okay. Will you see that they get back?" He said, "Yeah."

Mike was working the next day with McGuire. I said, "You tell him that we got these nuns and we didn't know whether they were women or men or not, so Herman lifted up their skirts to see if they were women." So he told this to McGuire. He went out of his mind. He said, "You did that to a *nun*?"

You know, they didn't have full mustaches, but a lot of hair. But anyway, we got that straightened out.

ROY RICH
Captain, Fraternal Order of Police

I was with one of my first partners, Carl Barnett. We had a complaint as we were driving past a house on East 78th Street. A lady flags us down and tells us her neighbor is at it again.

We knock on the door and she comes to the door and says, "I got my headache. I got a headache again." We had seen this lady wearing a tinfoil hat, out sweeping her walkway every day. People are quirky. She said, "I wore my tinfoil hat, but it doesn't stop the

---

She said, "I wore my tinfoil hat, but it doesn't stop the rays from coming in my head anymore."

---

rays from coming in my head anymore."

I said, "You have just one layer of tinfoil? You know that doesn't work anymore. They have special things now. You need to put a layer of tinfoil, then wax paper, then tinfoil. It's like a special resistor, but you need to put it inside another hat. Inside a cloth hat." She said, "Okay, okay."

We'd see her out there. She was wearing an old fishing hat and sweeping her walk every day. She was fine. No more headaches. Never complained to us again. That was the way things were done 20 years ago. Today we have a lot more resources. We'd try to get her some medical help. But that was exactly what she needed. We'd drive by and we'd wave at her.

FRANK BOVA, JR.
Sergeant, Third District

When I was in the Third District, we arrested a guy for disorderly conduct in the Flats. We had to take him all the way to the Sixth District because the Third didn't have a jail in it and the Justice Center was full.

The guy is telling us, "I want a test. You did not give me a test. I want a test." We get out of the car and we're waiting for the door to open and he says, "I want a test." I said, "Okay, hop on one foot and sing the alphabet." So he starts hopping on one foot singing the alphabet. He didn't do too bad. But that's not what he was under arrest for. He was under arrest for fighting and disorderly conduct. So he got done and I said, "You know something? You passed. You've got to be in for disorderly conduct because nobody else would do what you just did."

MARGARET DORAN
Patrol Officer, Mounted Unit

We were at the new Browns stadium. They had a soccer game there. It was the first world-class soccer game in Cleveland to be held in 10 years. And it was the Scotsmen versus the Argentineans. So I'm working with a Puerto Rican officer named Dave Cortez. I said, "I get to root for the Scotsmen. You get to root for the Argentineans." Of course, the Scotsmen won. I met several lovely, charming people. The Irishmen and the Scotsmen had bagpipes and there was a lot of beer involved—for them, anyway.

We had to stand by and watch. But, I'll tell you what, when they came out of that stadium and all those Irishmen and Scotsmen were a little under the weather from all they had to drink, I got 17 proposals of marriage—and the horse got 9. I'll tell you what, they're lining up and they're going, "You're beautiful, darlin'. Would you marry me?" I said, "The man who just left, I think I'm engaged to him."

JOE SADIE
Captain, Cops for Kids Program

You learn lessons on the police department and they stay with you for your lifetime. Look at this hand. You know what that's from? I shot myself. I had a gun just like this one, an automatic, under my bed.

I had just gotten married, about three or four months before. I was having a platoon party for the Sixth District over at my house— a pretty house off of Schaaf Road, with a swimming pool. So, we were cooking beans. And I'm thinking about that gun upstairs. My wife's going to be cleaning under the bed, and this and that. The automatic weapon I always kept there was all right because I lived by myself. I was a little askew because that was also the day my wife told me—now here I am, almost 40 years old—and my wife tells me that we were having twins. I was single all my life, no kids, and I'm going to have two. And obviously, it was on my mind.

So I left the kitchen and I go upstairs, and I get the automatic weapon. I looked at it and took it in the other room. I see that it's got rust on it. So, I'm thinking, "Well, I've got to clean this. I'm going to take it apart." I don't know what I was thinking. I just know my mind was somewhere else, obviously. It was half-cocked with a bullet in the chamber. It was a .45 Colt, army gun. I'm looking down the barrel of it and the trigger wouldn't go forward. I couldn't pull the trigger. I said, "Oh yeah." I turned the gun away and I had my hand dangling over the end of the barrel and I said, "That's cuz you have to pull the hammer all the way back." This is what I'm thinking, and then pull the trigger—it had a double-safety—which I did, and which I commenced to blow my hand apart. And I was bleeding like a pig. It looked like a can where you stick an M-80 in it and you blow it out. That's how my hand looked, all the gas, all the powder. It blew everything. It just blew it apart. Four operations it took to make it look like this.

So later on I asked my wife, "Did you hear that noise?" She said, "Yeah." She never came upstairs. She said, "I knew you did something wrong, but I didn't know what to do." But it wouldn't have mattered because I wasn't up there very long. I was like a rabbit, down the stairs, bleeding like a pig all over the place. And I ran into the kitchen and I grabbed a towel. I said, "Turn all this shit off. I shot myself. You've got to get me to the hospital." I wrapped up my hand, turned everything off, got into the car with her. I said, "You've got to drive."

So we're driving. "Go right here, go left here." We were going to Deaconess Hospital. "Honey, you're doing well. Take deep breaths. You're doing fine. Don't worry about the lights. We're going through the lights." This way, that way. "Turn left here." That's the way we bring people in on emergencies when I'm working. We pull in, park the car, go through the door. Me and her are coming into the hospital. The Emergency Room people start running toward us, grab my wife, put her in a wheelchair and took her away. So I yell, "Not her! Me!" That's how bad she was. She was a wreck.

They took me into the back room and they start working on my hand. And you know how it is—a policeman in a shooting. They've got to call the police. Internal Affairs show up. They thought it was domestic. I just got married. They thought maybe she shot me. I was going through all of that. My father-in-law, who was alive at the time, was deputy chief of Shaker Heights. You know how you transpose the story 50 times—how it changes. It went from Sergeant Sadie shot himself in the hand, to Sergeant Sadie shot himself in the head. So my poor father-in-law—and I loved that man—was headed to the hospital saying, "That son of a bitch just married my daughter, and that horse's ass shoots himself in the head."

His name was Joe Gardner. He went to church every morning. He was very religious. And he didn't call me a son of a bitch. That's what I used. He never swore. But horse's ass was the worst he'd ever said. So he got to the hospital . . . and he was relieved to find out I didn't shoot myself in the head.

Then there was a call to the hospital, and the next guy out on the list to be sergeant was hoping that I shot myself in the head. Because he would've gotten promoted to sergeant. They were telling me this story and I said, "Don't even tell me what his name is. Because I probably would've done the same thing."

TOM TUBE
Captain

We got called for a dead body, probable natural. We get there and it was. The guy passed away on the couch. So we call the morgue attendants to come and get the body and we're looking around the house while we're waiting for them.

We're waiting and waiting and waiting and waiting and still the morgue attendants aren't there. My partner, Ken Russell, used to work in the Third District before he came over to the Second. And he had a set of FM walkie-talkies. He bought them when he was working in the projects, where our portable radios had trouble transmitting and receiving.

So we're getting mad at having to wait and I said, let's put one of the radios under the couch, and when they go to move the body

> I said, let's put one of the radios under the couch, and when they go to move the body you be in the kitchen and say something.

you be in the kitchen and say something.

Well, the morgue attendants finally arrived an hour-and-a-half after they were called and they were drunk. It was just a real low-quality operation then. They came late; they were half in the bag.

They get the body bag and one guy grabs the corpse's shoulder and Kenny's in the kitchen and I'm thinking, "Here it comes . . ." And I was right.

Suddenly this voice cries, "Stop it! You're hurting me!" And they drop the body and yelled at me, "What was that?" I said I didn't know, and one of them said I was throwing my voice. I told him I didn't know how to throw a voice and then Kenny comes out of the kitchen and says, "If that guy's still alive, you better not take him."

But the body was dead and they started putting it in the body bag. Ken had gone back to the kitchen and now the attendants hear, "Hey, wait a minute! I can't breathe in here!" It was like a comedy routine. It was beautiful. After they left, we called our lieutenant in case a complaint was filed. We told him what we did and he said, "You guys are nuts."

MICHAEL DUGAN
Captain (retired), Cleveland; Chief of Police, Independence
Me and my partner stopped a guy driving downtown once. My partner is standing at the driver's side window and the guy said, "Do you know who I am?" And my partner said, "You're a fellow who went through a red light." The driver said, "Do you know that I work for ABC?" My partner responded, "That's okay because I work for CBS." And he said, "What do you mean, CBS?" And my partner said, "Carl B. Stokes."

MICHAEL DUGAN
Captain (retired), Cleveland; Chief of Police, Independence
There was a new officer in the Third District, the first day out of the academy, and an old-timer known for playing practical jokes. This would be in 1983, I believe, Third District. An older officer had a penchant for playing practical jokes and looked at the young officer and complimented him on his neat uniform. He kind of gave him a head to toe tweaking, and he observed that the officer really did kind of need a shoeshine to tip off the very crisp uniform. And

the officer admitted that he really would have liked to do something with his shoes but didn't get a chance today.

He directs him and says, "There's an old office that says on the door, 'Captain.' You'll find an old, bald-headed black fellow who wears a dark, navy blue jumpsuit. He's the janitor." In fact, it was Captain Ralph Burkes. He says to the young cop, "Just plop yourself down in the chair and tell the guy you need a shoe shine." Believe it or not, Captain Ralph didn't get mad. I think he said something to the officer like, "It must have been so-and-so that sent you."

ANDES GONZALEZ
Commander, Third District

If I wasn't working with Jim Simone, I was working with Dave Sumskis, may he rest in peace. He retired in his late fifties and passed away a couple years ago. Heart attack. He was 5 feet, 10 inches, 230 or 240. He was the fattest, fastest policeman I have ever seen. I used to tell him that.

He asked me to teach him some Spanish. I taught him to say, *muchas gracias*, or thank you. And *buenos dias*, or have a good day. We didn't have an opportunity for him to use them until one day we were at a Spanish home. When we were leaving, I said to them, "We're going to leave. We're car No. 213. If you need anything, give us a call. And my partner wants to tell you something."

Dave is smiling, then turning a bit red, then he says, "Blow your noses and mow your grasses." Turned out he froze up and he had made *muchas gracias* into "mow your grasses" to make it easier to remember. Same with *bueno dias*, "blow your noses." I had to explain to the family.

MIKE FRICK
Sergeant, Second District (retired)

I was in the Tactical Unit and we got a presidential detail for Jimmy Carter. I can't recall if he was campaigning or if it was later. I think it was his last year in office. Those details would last hours and hours. It wasn't anything to work 18 straight hours. You were briefed and assigned. You'd have to be in place two hours before Air Force One landed. There were guys at the airport and other guys would be at the hotel where he stayed.

Our assignment was the south stairwell of the Marriott at West 150th Street and I-71. The way they set it up was a vacant floor

---

I flipped the light on and who's laying there in his jammies but Jimmy Carter.

---

above the president and a vacant floor below him. They always had a Secret Service agent standing guard by or near the door. Every door had the key in it. If they had to get in there for one reason or another, the key was in there. All you had to do was turn the key and you were in the room. You'd have two guys above the floor and two guys below in the stairwell. Then you'd have guys at the elevator. These were usually Cleveland policemen who took care of this because these were the shit jobs.

After about 16 hours in a cold stairwell, I got relief, so I came downstairs. We were allowed to go to the command post and they had a coffee room set up. I came out of the stairwell and I'm walking down the hallway. I hadn't been there before and I had no idea where the command post was, but there was a Secret Service agent standing in front of this door.

The guy was asleep on his feet, and I mean sound asleep. I'm looking around and all the doors are closed, so I figured this was the command post. I turned the key and walked in and the room was dark. I flipped the light on and who's laying there in his jammies but Jimmy Carter.

With that, the Secret Service guy must have woke up. I looked at Jimmy Carter and said, "Nice jammies, Jimmy." I walked out, the Secret Service grabbed me and took me down to the command post and I got my ass chewed out. I told them, "How did I know?

Carter didn't sleep with a Mr. Peanut doll, like a lot of people said.

WILLIAM TELL
Commander, Sixth District (retired)

One evening I was in bed, and I wanted to get some sleep. I hear glass break downstairs. I wake up and I thought, maybe it's one of my girlfriends breaking the door down, thinking I have another girl in the house. Oh, yeah. You had plenty of girlfriends on the police department. Women love the uniform. So, I go down the stairs. And when I get downstairs, I had my gun in my hand and I could clearly see that it wasn't a girl, but it was an individual—a man's hands.

He had broken my back window and had thrown something at the door, and he was trying to get the deadbolt loose. He couldn't see me because the blind was down on the back door. He couldn't see me, but I'm standing, looking at him. So I got my gun in my hand and I'm in my shorts, no shoes on. Things go through your mind so fast in a situation like this—telling me to shoot the guy through the door. Being a young policeman and hearing all kinds of evidence they can use against you, I think, "No, I can't shoot this guy, because if I shoot him through the door, they might find glass fragments outside and see that he never got in. And if I shoot him through the door itself, the bullet might not penetrate." Things are going through your mind just that fast, and clicking through your mind. Then something tells you, grab his arm. No, he might pull me out. Hold him. Can't get to the telephone. These things are going through your mind real quick.

The last thing is, you better go out and get this guy. Yes, I better go get him. So I turned around and went upstairs to my bedroom. I don't want to cut the lights on because it'll scare him away. I put my police uniform on. I couldn't find my police shoes, so I got in my house shoes. And I went downstairs and did a search of the first floor of my house. Then I did a search of the basement of my house. The guy wasn't in the house. I went outside and looked for the guy. He's not on the back porch. But I heard something out there, "Go back. Go back."

So I turned and looked, and here, two males are standing in my driveway—on the sidewalk, in my driveway, motioning me to go back because the lady next door was coming home with her car. So I started to walk toward these individuals, and I had my police uniform on, but not until I came from the dark, out into the street-light, that they saw who I was. One guy ran and I shot at him and missed him. Hit the lady's house across the street. The next guy and I started to scuffle. And so I would hit him and he would fall in the snow. Then I would get him down—there was a lot of snow that winter, the tree lawns were full of snow. I would pull him out of the snow and we go scuffling and fighting.

The neighbors came out, begging me, "Mr. Tell, Mr. Tell, don't beat that man up. You better call the police." The guy tells me, "Yeah, call the police." I said, "Look, man, I *am* the police," and I showed him my badge. Then one of my girlfriends drove past. I said, "Go in the house and call the police for me while I've got this guy'" And the newspaper made an article the next day. The headline read, "Bumbling Burglar Picks the Wrong Home."

LEE ASHCROFT
Patrol Officer, Scientific Investigations Unit (retired)

Twenty-three of my 25 years were in SIU. Our unit consisted of the forensic lab, the fingerprint unit and the photo lab. We used Kodak Carousel 35 millimeter slide trays. You'd come in and we'd ask you the height, weight, what type of crime it was. And we'd look up in our cross-reference and we'd pull out our Carousels. And we checked on the screen color mug shots, slides, of people we've arrested in connection with crimes like that. And although it's not like Hollywood, where you'd get a hit every time somebody would come in, I have actually seen people pick out suspects and we went on to prosecute them. Of course at the same time, your office man, the third man on your platoon—two men went out on a run car and we had the whole city during the shift. If you were the office man during the day time and a victim would come in, you'd ask them, "Step in here, " and you'd sit them down and you put slides on.

We actually had it happen where we had somebody come in for a fingerprint for a passport, and we erroneously thought that they were there to look at slides [of suspects.] We took them into the room and we sat them down, and I don't know how we came up with a description, but about an hour-and-a-half later, they would say, "You know, I really don't know why I'm doing this, I'm here for fingerprints."

Or we had the one woman say, "Well, this is nice, but when are you going to show me the backs of the heads, because that's all I saw, the back of the head of the person who took my purse and ran."

MARGARET DORAN
Patrol Officer, Mounted Unit

All those years that I was growing up—I finally ended up being a cop on a horse—all those years, my father [also a cop] never took me to the Mounted Unit. All the other cops' kids got to see the horses. Not me. Not one, single time did he take me to see those horses. But I remember the day in front of the old Central Station. He was walking from the old data processing unit, across East 21st Street to Central Station to drop some stuff off. At the side steps there was a police horse tied to the railing. And my father petted the horse a couple of times. And he thought, "I see people feeding these horses all the time. What can I feed this little guy?" So he reached into his pocket and pulled out a brand-new bag of Hall's Mentholyptus, cherry flavored.

It turns out that, occasionally, these are given to the horses at the stables. They either, A) like the taste, or, B) it helps clear out their lungs a little bit when they have upper respiratory problems. And my father opened up this brand new bag and he opened one of these things up. And he fed it to the horse, and the horse gobbled it right up. So he opened a second one, and a third, and on and on and on. And by the time he was done, he had fed this horse the entire bag. Horses drool a lot. So what was in, was now running out in big, red, gooey gobs and running on the pavement like a faucet. My father walked away, laughing and laughing. He just knew that mounted guy was going to come out and figure his horse was bleeding to death.

* * *

I get on the elevator one day on the ground level of the Justice Center. I'm 8½ months pregnant. There are several people on the elevator. Some I know; some I don't. It goes up from the second level of the garage to the first level. The doors open up. The chief of police, Ed Kovacic, gets on in full uniform. The doors close. I only had a couple of floors to do my worst.

I put one hand on my big stomach and with the other, I pointed to the chief and said it was him. "He did this to me." Chief Kovacic was always a class act. He was absolutely mortified. He backed into a corner. He's a big man. He was a large presence. He backed into a corner and he got real pale and his voice got real tight.

And before anybody got off the elevator with the wrong impression, I tried to clarify. I said, "Chief, Chief. It was just a joke. Where's your sense of humor?" And he looked at me and he goes, "It wasn't funny, Doran." I said, "Wow, does that mean that I'll have a beat on the breakwall after I have this baby?" Every time I run into him at a public function that is one of the many stories he tells.

JEFF STANCZYK
Patrol Officer, Third District

Tony Colon and I were in this old lady's house. I was looking at her, and Tony was beyond her, behind her. So I could see Tony, but she can't see him. So, I'm looking at him. I'm taking the report and I'm watching him.

You know how old ladies dry their underwear on the heater? The old-lady underwear? Well, he's looking and he finds a pair of this underwear. I'm looking and looking and he's picking it up and he's dancing with it behind her. I'm looking at him and telling her, "I'm really sorry about your house getting broken into." And I'm looking at him and he's dancing.

But what he didn't know was, her granddaughter was sitting in the bedroom watching him dance with the underwear. So we got

---

But what he didn't know was, her granddaughter was sitting in the bedroom watching him dance with the underwear.

---

back to the district and they called. The boss said, "Well, why was your partner playing with this lady's underwear?" I'm like, "Well, it didn't happen like that. It fell off." It was a lie. He was dancing with it. He didn't put it on his head or nothing, but that was pretty funny.

TIM LEAHY
Sergeant, Third District
I've been on funeral detail since 1985. One of the final salutes we do is fire the rifles and then play "Taps." In 1987, we had a funeral at Holy Cross Cemetery. There were ducks flying overhead, and when we fired the rifles they pooped. It landed on our hats. Another time, the bugler was under a tree and the shots scared a squirrel so badly he fell out of the tree and knocked the bugle out of the bugler's hand.

MICHAEL DUGAN
Captain (retired), Cleveland; Chief of Police, Independence
We had an officer working off-duty in the early to mid-'70s in what they called the West Shore Security Patrol. People in the area around Harborview, Edgewater Drive with a little bit of money,

pooled their money and bought a car and an original car phone. They used them to make direct calls to the officer if they couldn't get their regular First District officers quick enough. The ones on this part-time detail would take care of it. They'd do extra services, like regular vacation checks, take in mail and stuff.

A resident, the Cleveland superintendent of schools, made a call to the off-duty officer and said, "I don't know. Somebody might be hurt. I hear screaming and moaning in the bushes behind the rear-most portion of my property."

The officer responds, and as he arrives on the scene he finds a young girl bent over, mounted by a young man. They're having sex, I guess it would be characterized as "doggy fashion," and during the whole time they're having sex, the individual is sipping a can of beer and putting it down and continuing, and sipping a beer.

The officer, obviously, breaks up the sexual encounter. In questioning the individual, he asks him where he works, and the guy said, "I'm a Cleveland Public School teacher." To which the officer said, "You asshole, you're screwing behind the Superintendent's house!"

10.

"That's our job."

[ODDS & ENDS]

SEAN GORMAN
Patrol Officer, Ports & Harbor Unit

It used to be really busy in the Flats, when all the bars and all the restaurants and stuff down there were open. It's dead now, but when I first got there, it was 1998. It was busy then. There'd be rows of boats 10 to 12 deep—fast boats. Then there'd be the big money boats. They would be three to four deep. There'd be a couple rows of those. You know, it used to be busy. It was a blast when I first started in the Harbor Unit down there. It was awesome. There were people everywhere.

I think we averaged about 10 bodies a year. That's bodies recovered; out of the water. We may not recover all of them. The fire department may get it. But locally, there was at least 10 bodies, I think, a year.

I got a kid behind Shooters. Summer of 1999, and hot. It was late at night. The victim, it was his 21st birthday. And my partner, Bill Kubiak, and I were going up to a club that had some complaints. We were staying late. And we get a call that there's a drowning at the old river bend behind Shooters. I was told they got drunk. They got kicked out of a number of places. This kid goes in the water with blue jeans and boots. He was going to swim across and try to swim back, or whatever. He's drunk. He's in the water.

So, I got my dive gear and my boat and go back around the corner. There's tons of people out. The Coast Guard shows up. An eyewitness says, "He went down right there." We set up and I went down. We drop a concrete bucket with a line coming to the surface. That's what we hang on to when we're under.

The Cuyahoga River is zero visibility. Everything we do is really fucked up. It's not like the Bahamas or Cancun. It's zero visibility. When you're in the river, you can't see anything. When you get to the bottom, it's like, you close your eyes and that's what you can see. It gives you a headache to sit there and look in the darkness.

A friend of mine said, "Close your eyes. You're not going to see anything anyway. Why sit there and kill your eyes trying to look at something?" So I do the same thing. I close my eyes and it works great.

So everything is touching. The first time, I go around in a circle, I don't find anything, and I'm all the way out. Finally I come back up and the witness says, "Maybe it's over here a little bit more." So the Coast Guard boat comes over and they drag it over. My partner asks me if I'm okay. I'm fine. I've got plenty of air. I drop back down into the water. And I mean, not even a quarter of a turn and I

When you're in the river, you can't see anything. When you get to the bottom, it's like, you close your eyes and that's what you can see.

---

found the kid's leg. I find the body. I find his leg and his foot. I said, "Okay, that's what I needed to find."

I know what it is. You can feel it. So I surface with him, and I take him to the other side of the river, away from Shooters. I went there because that's where the EMS is. They treat everybody as if they're still alive, even if he was in the water for a while. I'm not allowed to say he's dead. If you're in the water for 45 minutes or an hour, it's pretty sure you're dead. But I'm not allowed to say he's dead.

That was the first body I recovered. So I brought him up and they took him over to the EMS right away. That's our job. That's what we do.

JIM GNEW
Patrol Officer, SWAT

After I was working, I told my uncle, "You've got to get me in the motorcycle unit." I wanted to go to that unit really bad. He said, "All right, this is what I'll do. You spend five years out there in the Fourth, and one day after your fifth year I'll yank you. You can come down and work with me in the motorcycle unit."

So I strived for that. I worked for that day. And it finally arrived. By that time I was married and we were at a Knights of Columbus dance at St. Wenceslas in Maple Heights. My mom and dad were there. My uncle was there. We were all there. I walked up to him and said, "Listen, it's five years and one day today. So do I just come to the motorcycle unit tomorrow?"

He said, "Wait a minute. I have to talk to your wife." I said, "What are you talking about? I'm the man in the family, not her." He said, "You know what? If I do this, she's never going to talk to me again." I said, "No big deal" and he went and talked with her. To make a long story short, I didn't go to the motorcycle unit.

Later that year I went to see a sergeant in the chief's office. I played softball with the sergeant's son. I told him I couldn't go to the motorcycle unit and the only other unit I wanted was the Tactical Unit, which is now SWAT. But back then, the only way that you got in the Tactical Unit was to have already shot somebody. That way, they figured, if the shit hit the fan you wouldn't be turning and running away. I had been involved in one shooting at that point, so the sergeant said, "I'll see what I can do."

Time went by and one day he called me and said, "I think I can get you in. Are you ready?" That night I said to my wife, "You have two choices: I'm either going to the motorcycle unit," which she knew about, "or the Tactical Unit," which she didn't. It was the Tactical Unit.

JIM SIMONE

Patrol Officer, Traffic Unit, Second District

I give a lot of traffic tickets, but I also make a lot of other arrests. The two most common calls to radio all year long are speeders and loud music. People get pissed off about speeders on their street and they get pissed off about Joe Blow and his 5,000-amp system in his $50 car going down the street.

I'm the DUI guy. I do a lot of DUIs. I have a personal vendetta against DUIs. I almost got killed a couple years ago. A guy ran me off the freeway doing about 78 miles per hour. I was a prick before, but now I'm a super prick. If you've been drinking and I stop you, you're spending the night with me . . .

When I stop someone and find marijuana, I throw them in jail. I've seen officers take a bag of marijuana and stand in front of the car and say, "What did you pay for this?" The guy says $40. Then the officer opens the bag and lets the wind blow it all away and says, "You wasted $40, huh?" It's a simple citation, $500. Once you get stopped by me, your problems will compound themselves because I'm going to throw you in jail for driving under the influence of drugs, transporting drugs in your vehicle, and possession of drugs.

DENNIS SWEENEY

Detective, First District

When I first got to the Fourth, the drug was marijuana. We grabbed the guys running. They'd have ten little bags of marijuana. But when crack cocaine hit, I never saw anything like it.

At one point, because we were pretty good workers—myself and a guy named Damian Glazer—they made us a fast response car. He's a sergeant now in the Third District. He's kind of a big guy. But they made us a fast response car, where all we handled were Priority One runs, and when we weren't on that, we handled drug stuff. The guys off of East 93rd Street got to know us. So they would just move their operation from one block to the next block to the next block.

Back then, they would have a pill bottle full of rocks of crack cocaine and just carry it in their pocket. Then as it kind of moved on, they started getting ingenious where they were hiding the stuff. And eventually it went to where they were hiding it in their mouth. They would wrap it in cellophane, and if they had to they would swallow it. Now they hide it up their ass. They hide it everywhere.

But I've never seen a drug take over like crack. In 1987 we closed one of the first drug houses down in that district. That's when Cleveland came up with that law that they boarded up the drug houses. They ended up razing the house. We did a raid one day for the news media.

I've seen guys on heroin and coke, but that crack is just bad stuff. Even since I've been on the west side, all the robberies we handled, it was always drug addicts on crack, because they just need it, need it, need it. You know, in ten minutes, you're done. You need more. It's a bad drug.

* * *

Had a guy who lives in the inner city with some drug issues and who was arrested for drugs. He wanted his car back, because apparently they towed his car. He was threatening to jump from the Lorain Avenue Bridge. So I told him we could get his car back. It worked. He was getting his car back anyway because the dope they took from him, they call them dummies, they were wax. They weren't actually crack cocaine.

If it was real crack, they could've confiscated the car on behalf of the city. He was selling fake crack. These guys that are bad on the crack, they sell dummies. They'll take peanuts and cut them up. They'll take candle wax, soap, whatever they can. They'll sell it and get the money and take off. Very dangerous.

On the east side in the Fourth District, a guy got his head blown off for that, a shotgun. And he was a regular kid from the neighborhood that was selling, slinging. He must've gotten on the shit and he got killed later. He sold to the wrong guy, the wrong stuff and they pow'ed him.

DENNIS WONDRAK

Patrol Officer, Fourth District

We pulled a guy over for a traffic violation. He ran a red light and had no driver's license. After the guy got out of his car, I looked on the floor and saw a little plastic baggy, you know, crack cocaine. It was pretty smashed up. He must have been stepping on it or something. I showed my partner. We had the guy in the back seat of the zone car. I said to him, "Hey, what's on the floor," and he said, "That crack cocaine wasn't mine!" That was an easy bust. I didn't ask him about crack cocaine or drugs. All I asked was, "What's on the floor?"

ELIAS DIAZ

Sergeant, Police Academy

Every time you think you've seen it all, something new arrives. I was working at the First one day and this guy comes in, pretty upset. He tells me he parked his car with the keys in it when he ran into a store for a pack of cigaretes. When he came out, the car was gone. He called his cell phone in the car and the thief answered it. He told the victim he could have his car back for $500, but first, the thief was going to Crazy Horse to watch dancing girls and have a few drinks. We went a couple guys down there, and the guy's stolen car was in the parking lot. Pretty soon out comes the car thief. Out of the Crazy and into handcuffs.

JOE SADIE

Captain, Cops for Kids Program

In 1973, I got the Rotary Award for Heroism, above and beyond the call of duty. I was a patrolman in the Second District, and we were having a rash of Lawson's store holdups. Those were, like, quick money exchange for robbers. If they needed money, they would go in there and they would just rob the store. There were a chain of Lawson's stores.

There was a guy in the month of November that had robbed 19 stores in 23 days. And we had lots of holdups so they would hire off-duty policemen to stand in the back of the store. There were several instances where the guys would come in the back door and stick the gun in the policeman's face. They had one where they put the gun in the policeman's face and the policeman pulled his gun out and shot and killed him. The policeman said later that he thought he was dead anyway. But that's how bad it was. They would hire off-duty Cleveland policemen with the rash of robberies. Then the robberies would stop. Then they'd start up again. Some stores would hire policemen. Then they'd start putting cameras in. Then we would have details outside of stores waiting for them to get robbed. This was very, very prevalent back in the '70s.

So here we have a picture of a Lawson's holdup. A man that was somewhat tall, wearing a three-quarter-length jacket with a gray bottom and a black velvet collar. But what was significant—this was kind of a common coat at that time. But what was significant in the picture—we all had pictures; they handed out 100 pictures—there was a button missing. The third button was missing on his coat. He was walking out of the door and his coat was buttoned up, but the third button was missing.

I used to work part-time security at Carousel Bowling Alley, at Ridge Road and Denison Avenue. I walked in and out and I did the parking lot. And here's this guy walking past me. And something about him is familiar. What's familiar is the coat, the picture. Not the guy's face, that third button that I memorized. If I ever see a coat with a third button missing, take a look and see if it's this guy. So I pulled the picture out of my pocket, and sure enough, it looks like this is the guy.

I was in uniform, but alone. He passed me up and goes into the pool hall. He gets a rack with the balls and he starts shooting pool. And I turned around and I gotta go back and look, because I don't want to call radio. The worst thing I want to do is make a false call. You look stupid. You bring everybody down and it's not the guy. It makes you look like an idiot. And especially if it's a customer that's there to patronize the place. So I wanted to be sure. So I go back and I look. He had the coat off, and I really can't see it too good.

But I noticed that I'm making him nervous because I'm staring at him.

So I thought to myself, "I'm just going to walk through one time and see if I can get a better look at the coat. So I go back in and I get a better look at the coat. I get a better look at him, and I make the decision that this is the guy. Even though the picture was blurry. I make the decision. I'm saying it's him. I'm going to arrest this guy. I'm going to call for backup because this guy who's been holding up these places is armed. And I don't want to [do] anything in the pool room because if he pulls a gun out and I get into a fight with him in there, he's going to kill somebody or I might shoot somebody trying to defend myself.

So I call for backup. The closest are these two coppers in a plainclothes detail. In the meantime what's happening is this guy decides that I stared at him too much. He puts his coat on and he's leaving. So as he's leaving, I'm walking back from the telephone—I've been watching him—to the exit of the pool hall. Here he comes out and I've got to make my move. So just as he's walking past me, he puts his hand in his pocket. And I reach for my gun and I grabbed his hand in his pocket. And I stick my gun in his chest, and I tell him not to move.

And about ten seconds later, here comes a barrage of policemen. And we get this guy arrested. And I'll tell you what I noticed. I know this sounds terrible. I pulled his hand out of his pocket. He's got the gun. And I check his other pocket, nothing. And I stand there staring at him, looking at the front of him, we're searching him, and he's got a humbly little hard on. I'm thinking this guy's all excited that he got caught. They say some of these guys want to get caught. This guy's got a hard on. I don't say nothing, or think nothing of it.

We get him to the station. The whole time he's denying he's the guy. He's not the guy. He's not the guy. And even the policemen that assisted me said he's not the guy, "Sadie, this isn't the guy. That's not enough, just the button on his coat." I said, "Yeah, but it looks so much like him." They say, "No, no, no. It's not the guy." We get him to the booking window. I go into the district. I got him at the booking window. They're asking him information. He's cooperating 100 percent. And now I'm thinking to myself, do I got the wrong guy, and is this guy going to make a complaint on me?

We got his picture hanging up at the booking window, so everybody we bring in we look to see if this guy that we're booking looks like the suspect. That's how bad we wanted him. So I thought I'd use a little psychology. "It's too bad you're not the guy, because the guy—you see his picture up here? See how I'm carrying his picture?—this guy's going to be famous. He's going to be on TV. The media's looking for him. This guy's unbelievable."

And I really sent a little smoke up his ass that this guy was going to be a celebrity. He confessed.

BILLY EVANS
Detective, Auto Theft (retired)
The majority of police work was pretty good. You had your good days and your bad days in police work. Luckily, the twenty-and-a-half years that I was on the job, I spent very little time in zone cars. Most of my time was spent in specialized units, like auto theft or Tac Unit or detective. But being a detective in Cleveland, you don't get any extra fee. It's not considered as a promotion. You're still, in reality, just a patrolman.

KEVIN GRADY
Patrol Officer, Fourth District
It was the middle of December, 2001. There had been a series of violent robberies and assaults in the Warner and Turney roads area, the southernmost section of the Fourth District.

My partner, Mike Urbania, and I went undercover. We became installers with a television cable truck and set up shop in the street. Because we had made arrests in the area before, we also wore wigs and false teeth. We spent a lot of our time on Warner Road, putting up and taking down traffic cones, pretending to splice cable. We didn't know who we were looking for. All we knew was that it was four or five black males and the victims were white. And we knew it was racially motivated, but we didn't have much to go on.

At one point, several black males started walking around our truck. We wondered if they were planning to rob us. They got very comfortable. They even came up to us and asked if we could sell them cable boxes. They were selling drugs within 15 feet of us.

Then one day, we were standing by the truck and we heard one of the guys talk about beating a victim so severely that "he was on his hands and knees begging for his life." We realized these were the guys we were looking for. Now the victims lived in that same neighborhood with the suspects and the victims were so scared of retribution that they didn't want to press charges.

With some encouragement, though, the victims identified the suspects. One of the victims was mentally handicapped. They took seven dollars and a case of beer from him. They beat him so bad they broke one of the bones around his eyes. Now he's blind in one eye. They broke his arm, jaw and ribs. Another victim, a woman, temporarily lost her hearing as a result of the beating. They were dragging her into the street when she wouldn't let go of her purse. When they were beating and kicking the victims, the suspects were yelling at them, "This is our street, you white motherfucker!"

We try to protect them, and the suspects are right back on the street. How could anyone in their right mind let these guys out of jail?

We got warrants for two of them. We found them walking down Warner Road near Goodman Avenue. When the leader saw me and Detective Phil Habeeb, he panicked. We had arrested him a few times before. We got a confession from one. He went into such great detail about every blow, kick and hit. The two juveniles turned themselves in. The 17-year-old was the big hitter, 6-foot-2 and 220.

Juvenile court released both of them four days later because, they said, no weapons were involved. The court didn't contact us. Matter of fact, we found out from a victim who called us. What are we supposed to tell the victims? We try to protect them, and the suspects are right back on the street. How could anyone in their right mind let these guys out of jail?

ROBERT LEGG
Lieutenant, Third District (retired)

Probably summer of 1972, nights. Mike Burger and I responded to a run at 114 and Woodland. That part of Woodland was an Italian community then. A car had pulled into a drive and bumped the owner's car. The driver was lying in the front seat, feigning unconsciousness. I covered while Mike opened the door and slowly pulled the occupant out. The male acted drowsy. Mike placed his hand on top of the car and started to pat him down. The action started.

The male spun trying to catch Mike on the throat with a ju-jitsu strike. Turns out he had been stationed in Korea in the military and had studied karate. He had bet his friends he could whip any two policemen. Across the street was a car loaded with his pals watching the "fun" take place.

He picked on Mike and me. That posed a small problem, Mike had boxed golden gloves, wrestled in college, and just been discharged from the Marines and a tour in Nam. I was studying Ki-KaJu Kempo—developed by Al Gene Carulia, grand national karate champion—a style utilizing kempo karate, judo and akido.

When we entered the booking area I was sure the sergeant would tear us up. He looked at the man and said, "What happened to him?" The man replied, "I fell." Then, looking at us, he said, "I'm a man. I asked for it, I got it. I'll live with it."

MIKE FRICK
Sergeant, Second District (retired)

It was late '70s. Phil Parish and I were partners. We had a good caseload and we had to go to court. We pulled a mayoral detail for the morning. You just sit your ass in front of the [mayor's] house and make sure nobody blows up the house, I guess. Phil went in the morning to court for preliminary hearings and grand jury. He was going to come back and relieve me because we had a trial that was supposed to start at 1:00 P.M.

I get all my folders and I'm sitting in the car and it was right around noon. The kid next door was Puerto Rican Joe. Everybody knew him because he worked at Clark Auto Parts and he was a nice guy and he comes out and asks, "You want a pop? You want a coffee?" Because those Kuciniches, they wouldn't give you shit. You could sit there and if you had to take a leak, you wet your pants before . . .

So I'm sitting there going over the statements and testimony and out of the corner of my eye I catch Sandy Kucinich. I look up and nod at her and went back to reading. I look back up and she's still standing there and I'm thinking, "What the hell?"

She's got the dog on the leash. She goes down the street. She comes back. She goes in the house. Next thing I know, she walks out and I'm still reading. I'm not paying attention to her. She comes over to the car and I roll down the window and I say, "Yes, Mrs. Kucinich, what can I do for you?"

She says, "How come you didn't get out of the car?" I say, "I've got a court case that I'm preparing for and I want to go in there and be—" She says, "Well, you were supposed to get out of the car and walk the dog for me." I looked at her and said, "What do you mean, walk the dog? That's not my job to walk the dog." She looks at me and she says, "You're to get out of the car and to walk the dog next time I come out."

I said, "With all due respect, I'm not walking your dog." And she said, "Well, you don't show me the respect I deserve. I'll have your job." I looked at her and by that time I knew I was in trouble. I said,

"I give you all the respect in the world, but I ain't walking your dog, so you can go fuck yourself."

With that, she goes in. Man, the shit hit the fan. She goes in and calls her husband, her husband calls the safety director, the safety director calls the lieutenant. She said I was sleeping on the job. I

I said, "With all due respect, I'm not walking your dog."

---

had a lieutenant, a sergeant, two detectives down there. Little did she know that when she walked the dog, a woman who owned a pizza shop came up the street and I waved to her because I knew her, too. She went, picked up her kids at school, she came back, had her kids with her and I waved at them and hit the siren for the kids. So now, when the siren went, Puerto Rican Joe came out of the house, walked over and started joking with me. He said, "Do you want any coffee?" I said, "No, I don't want any coffee," so he went back in.

In the meantime, I had picked up the radio and asked to have a car relieve me so I could get to court and prepare for the case because it was getting right around twelve o'clock and I wanted to get down there as I had a one o'clock case. So, Mrs. Kucinich goes in.

I get this call. They take me back to the Justice Center. Next thing I know, I get this, "Oh, you're going up on charges for sleeping."

Well, Bobby Gallagher was the inspector at the time. I explained it all to him. So he got the tapes—the radio tapes are all time-stamped—and he had the tapes analyzed at Case Western Reserve. The guy who analyzed them said, "There's no way this guy was sleeping between the times Mrs. Kucinich said he was sleeping."

Needless to say, you can't fight the Police Department, so I kind of threatened them a little bit with going to the newspapers and they finally said, "Well, we're not going to put you up on charges as long as you ask for a transfer." I said, "Okay, I want to go to Homicide." They wouldn't give me that, so I went back to the Second District because I found out that they were decentralizing the detective bureau in three or four months anyway and moving them into the districts.

ROBERT CERBA
Lieutenant, Fraternal Order of Police

A couple years ago I came into work at the Second District and found out about a very unusual homicide. Benjamin Mercato got executed on West 58th Street and Clark Avenue. He was set up. They threw him out of the house, put a gun to the back of the head and killed him.

A couple days later, Keith Scharf, from Ports and Harbors called me. He's a lieutenant. And he called me and tells me one of the suspects told Homicide that the murder weapon was thrown in the lake. I told him that I do metal detecting as a hobby. That's what I do. I've got water and land metal detectors. I could meet our Ports and Harbor guys down at Edgewater right by Perkins Beach. I met these guys down there. I took my equipment down and I showed them how to use it.

Only about waist deep water, but it's in the water nonetheless. From what they got from the person who threw the guns in—he had taken the guns down there and stood on a little knoll overlooking the lake and just heaved the guns out into the lake. So we had an idea as to what area they were in. So I showed the Ports and Harbor guy how to use my metal detector.

The one I took down there works up to 250 feet under the water. So I go down there and I showed them how to use it. I gave them a 5- or 10-minute show on how to do it, but unless you do it constantly, you move slow. I noticed they were having problems, doing it real slow.

So I said, "I'm going to get my stuff and come back." All that I had was a wet suit and this, of course, was November and it was really cold. So I went out in the water and it was real cold. And I started searching. I was in the water approximately half an hour when I found the first gun. And about 20 minutes later I found the second gun. We turned them over. We called Homicide immediately. They came out and looked at the guns. They had SIU out there. They photographed everything. They took them down and Nate Wilson, who is in our Scientific Investigation Unit, the resident gun expert down there, he's the one that does all the test firing and everything else. He took the guns down to our range, where they took them apart. They took all sand out of them that had been there, and started test firing the guns. And after a couple of test fires, where it cleaned any residual rust out of the barrel, he was able to get a positive match to the bullet that killed Benjamin Mercado.

And the suspects, at the time, never knew that we had recovered the guns, until they were getting ready to go to trial. And once their attorney found out, both of the suspects pled out . . . So it sewed up and cleared up that homicide permanently.

MIKE O'MALLEY
Detective, Homicide Unit (retired)

We assisted another car that was stopping a guy at Chester and Crawford Avenues. I'm watching from behind. The guy's hand is going up when the officer grabbed it. The man was wearing a wig, and under the wig was a .357 Magnum. He was reaching for a gun. That was one thing that stuck in my mind very well. This is what they taught us in the academy: With a gun, it's the one you don't find that's going to kill you.

JEFF STANCZYK
Patrol Officer, Third District

One of the proudest moments I ever had was after Rodney King got all beat up [in Los Angeles.] We didn't touch him, and yet, the coppers would be catching the flack for it, just because you're a policeman. And there were a bunch of kids coming down the street. They were from Cleveland State or whatever. And they had a big banner, a big sheet. And it said on that sheet, "Come to Cleveland and be Treated Like a King." They were all black kids. So if you come to Cleveland and you're black, you're going to get your ass kicked, is what the sign meant. And they're coming down the street, saying, "Come to Cleveland and be treated like a King. Come to Cleveland and be treated like a King."

I'm looking; there had to be 50 kids there. There was an old copper directing traffic at Ontario Street and St. Clair Avenue. There was construction or something going on there that day. So I pulled the car over and I'm standing next to this cop. And these kids were as close as I am to you. They stopped right there. They're looking at this cop and they're going, "Come to Cleveland and be treated like a King." And the copper walked up to the kids.

He took his hat off and he said, "I'll treat you like a King." He said, "I'll treat you like Martin Luther King would've wanted me to treat you." He put his hat on, he turned around, and those kids said nothing. He caught them so flat-footed with what he said. You saw them pass back what he said to that group, and they turned around and they marched back up St. Clair Avenue. One guy diffused 50 people just like that because he knew what to say.

DANNY CONNORS
Patrol Officer, First District

I saw a car that I knew was reported stolen. The guy went ahead and led us on a little chase. It probably only lasted 40 seconds. He pulled in a driveway and jumped out. The car crashed into the garage, so I jumped out and started chasing the guy. I chase him three blocks, catch [him] in a backyard, get my gun out and order him to put his hands up. This was around East 108th Street and Aetna Avenue.

He starts coming at me, so I put my gun away. He doesn't have a weapon in his hand. I get my asp—it's an expandable baton. A wood baton would have worked better because it's made of oak—it's not hollow like the asp. I start hitting him with the asp and the asp collapses. We're going at it, a good couple of minutes. I get him on the ground and I ended up getting him handcuffed.

I couldn't call for help because my portable had detached from my belt. So it's just me and this guy in the backyard. An old man comes up to me, hands me my portable and says, "Are you all right?" I said yes, I was. He said, "Know what you should have done, sonny? You should have picked up that two by four over there and cracked him over the head. That would've helped."

It was just kind of surprising because he was an elderly black gentleman and the suspect was black and every time I've been in a situation like that it's made to sound like I'm out beating people for no reason.

ANDES GONZALEZ
Commander, Third District

The thing that struck me about police work was that, in wearing a badge, you're almost like a magnet. And what I mean by that is that you're not necessarily looking for something to happen, but

---

Wearing a badge, you're almost like a magnet.

---

yet, you're always looking for something. You're looking for crime to happen. And you could be out looking for a car thief and the next thing you know, you're chasing a guy who was burglarizing a house. So that's what I learned real quick. Expect the unexpected.

RICHARD SICHAU
Patrol Officer, Third District (retired)

I was in the Third District when the Hough riots started. We rushed over and right into sniper fire at Hough Avenue and East 75th Street. Somebody got the bright idea to shoot out the street-lights so we weren't such easy targets. We were behind our cars when a police car comes down the street, driving slowly with lights on. We yelled and the lights went out. The door opened and out walked Chief Richard Wagner. He said, "I wanted to see what was going on and how you handle this situation."

LEE ASHCROFT
Patrol Officer, Scientific Investigations Unit (retired)

A guy was sawing pipes out of an old railroad roundtable house off of St. Clair Avenue. He was a bandit, and it was a typical, copper-pipes-out-of-the-basement thing. So it was 10:30 and we were due off, and Earl had a previous commitment. And he started being flustered because he couldn't make the commitment. He said, "Can you type?" I said, "Sure, I can type." He said, "Can you do the report and I'll book the prisoner?" I said, "Fine."

Well, at that time, I got back and started typing like a madman. And three-quarters of the way through the report, I was positive that someone was standing behind me and it was Sergeant Jack Burns, one of the three sergeants that we had on our shift, holding a cigarette Russian-style in his right hand and leaning against the wall. And he said, "So, we have us a typist in the Third District." And that's how I got to be the third man in the office. That's how I ended up upstairs in SIU, the scientific investigation unit, where I stayed for 23 years.

MICHAEL DUGAN
Captain (retired), Cleveland; Chief of Police, Independence

I was a lieutenant in the Third District, about 1988. There was me and another lieutenant. We had a sergeant who often found himself in trouble. The sergeant was complaining to me that the other lieutenant was always picking on him and finding fault with him. And my reply was, "Well, you can get along with him if you just obey the rules and don't get into trouble with him."

And I asked, "What is he picking on you for?" And he said, "Well, you know, yesterday night they were setting up for the Bud 500 at Burke Airport. I had my car; I had to see how well I could do. So I was out there doing about 105, 108 miles an hour. And the sergeant climbs all over me for that."

And he just couldn't understand why he was being set upon.

He had another incident that became legend and hit the local papers. At the time, he was a Second District sergeant. He drove down to the West Bank of the Cuyahoga River in the Flats. The Goodtime II was going down the river with Mayor Voinovich, members of City Council, and I think the city directors. They saw him fishing on duty. Right next to car 210, or whatever it was. And his story was—at his disciplinary hearing—that he went down and was talking to the business owner who was fishing in the river. The business owner's phone rang, he went to answer it and said, "Here, hold this," and at that very moment, the council and the mayor came down. He was given two weeks suspension for that infraction.

Later he was demoted to patrolman and assigned to the City Jail and the Justice Center. To show that he may have lost his stripes but not his sense of humor, behind the booking desk he had had his stripes and they were framed, encircled with a slash through them.

* * *

There used to be old-time desk sergeant in the Fourth District. He had a heart of gold. On Christmas Eve, he would take the individual prisoners out of their cells, handcuff them to a chair, buy a case of beer, let them watch TV and drink beer with him on Christmas Eve. He was really a good guy. He felt that nobody should have to stay totally out of touch at Christmas.

KYLE STOUGES
Patrol Officer, Third District

You need a little gratification from time to time, otherwise you get real salty. If someone is courteous to me, I will not write them a ticket. If they have a license and everything else—if they treat me with respect, if they're courteous, I give them the gift with open arms. "There you go, have a nice day." But as soon as they start getting ticked off and shouting the usual, "I pay your salary" stuff, I say, "Do you live in the city of Cleveland?" And when they say no, I tell them, "Well, I do. I pay my own salary."

JOE SADIE
Captain, Cops for Kids Program

Usually it was a Friday night in the Second District, early in my career. It was this thing that we had about the hillbillies on the near West Side. There were tremendous bars up and down Lorain Avenue and West 25th Street. The thing with the hillbillies was that they had to accomplish three things or they would turn into were-wolves on Monday: they had to get drunk; they had to get laid; and they had to get into a fight before the weekend was up. And it was, like, they lived up to that pattern. And then everybody you arrested was from West-by-God-Virginia, Logan County. It was like a standing joke. We had them at the booking window. We would look at them and then say, "What part of West Virginia are you from?" It sort of surprised them. They would say, "How did you know I was from West Virginia?" And we would say, "You're all from West Virginia."

WILLIAM TELL
Commander, Sixth District (retired)

We had a hundred-and-some people on the platoon [shift]. It was segregated, blacks working in one area of the district, white officers working in another area. And we had black police officers who couldn't work in certain areas. We couldn't work on Buckeye. We couldn't work on Shaker Square. We couldn't work Broadway. We had to work Kinsman, Mt. Pleasant. That wasn't written down; it was unofficial. I didn't have any problems with it because it was a job for me. Later on, you look at it and think, "Yeah, that wasn't right." But at that time, I just wanted to blend in and make some money.

JAMES MCMANUS
Patrol Officer, Impound Unit

Most of the time that I encountered racism, it was with people who were intoxicated. The funny thing, it wasn't so much that it just came from Caucasian people, a lot of it came from Hispanics and from African Americans. A lot of African-American suspects, or people that you questioned, they seemed to take the approach that, being an African-American policeman, you didn't know anything, that they always had to speak to the white officer.

My first year out there, I didn't understand it, but some of the older guys did. And after a while, it didn't faze me anymore. The white officers got their share of name-calling from Hispanic and black people. They were all called rednecks and honkies and all. Anything people could say to you that was derogatory of your race, they would say it. I took it personally, but eventually, I saw that it was directed at everybody. And I learned to just ignore it. My first encounter with it, I didn't. I didn't sleep well.

* * *

I've had some people write some letters to thank me for some of the things I've done, and I've kept them on my desk and put them in a frame. They don't really do anything as far as for your

> **A lot of people think you're a bad policeman when you're doing things that they don't like, like giving them a ticket.**

job, but personally-wise, they help. It kind of offsets—when you get the one nice letter, when you get the 20 people cussing you out calling you a bad cop. A lot of people think you're a bad policeman when you're doing things that they don't like, like giving them a ticket. If they don't park in the right place, you've got to give them a ticket. They can't stay there. But that same person, when he gets home and someone breaks in their house, they want that same cop to come over and help them out. So you can't play favorites. When you get there and you see that this is the same lady that cussed you out, you've got to go there and help them. I would say there's not a policeman who wouldn't.

ALAN CIELEC
Patrol Officer, First District (retired)

You go to roll call and you got 15 officers at roll call. That doesn't mean you have 15 officers who get along with each other. There's always a couple who see it different ways. You know, "Oh, I gotta work with her, or him, tonight?" They probably thought the same of me lots of times because I was aggressive and I wanted to pull over the whole neighborhood. Because in the area I worked, they were all low-lifes anyway. They all deserved to go to jail.

PETE MIRAGLIOTTA
Patrol Officer, Fourth District

[There's] the camaraderie and the stress that you blow off together, when you go out drinking, and you do the stupid shit like sit under the bridge and shoot rats.

Some of this craziness, I think that's where you blow that kind of stress off so you can deal with them, which is why, unfortunately, we drink too much, we probably overeat, we cheat on our wives . . . Because if you think about how much shit we do put up with—the general public and our own politicians and our own bureaucracy—the assholes on the street never bothered me. I always thought they were comical. They never bothered me. As you go along, most of the guys and gals—and I really believe this— probably get more frustrated with the bureaucracy and the politicians and the newspapers than they ever do with anybody on the street.

DENNIS WONDRAK

Patrol Officer, Fourth District

The things that bother me most are retired men and women having to deal with gangbangers, children in a house that's a mess and seeing animals get hurt. I hate to see people victimized, but the bottom line is, you get past it real quick. You get calloused. Otherwise, you're not going to survive.

BILL SPELLACY

Lieutenant, Fourth District (retired)

It's the best job I ever had. They gave me clothes to wear and a car to drive around in and no time clock. A bunch of good guys to work with. No mental giants, because if you were a genius, you wouldn't be a policeman.

Acknowledgments

The team that put together this book is a small one, but without those team members, there would be no book.

Donna Crockett carefully transcribed every audio tape I sent her and returned the transcripts to me for editing. I tell people not just about her dependable, professional way of working but about a comment she made. "Since I started transcribing these tapes," she said, "I've changed the way I feel about the police."

Editor Jan Leach started her journalism career—a long time ago—as a police reporter. When the huge and sloppy pile of copy was ready, I dropped it into her very capable hands. When she finished with it, the manuscript had become a book.

As usual, it was women who made me look good.

Finally, I'll always be grateful to the men and women who decided to sit and think about my questions . . . and answer them.